Jocelyn Galsworthy

LORDS OF CRICKET

For my father Jack (JN) Kendall
and my brother Johnny

Judy Vigors

Jocelyn Galsworthy

LORDS OF CRICKET

Players, Personalities and Legends

Words by Judy Vigors

SP

First published in the UK in 2005
by The Sportsman's Press, an imprint of Quiller Publishing Ltd

British Library Cataloguing-in-Publication Data
  A catalogue record for this book
  is available from the British Library

ISBN 1 904057 68 3

Printed in England by the University Press, Cambridge

The Sportsman's Press

An imprint of Quiller Publishing Ltd
Wykey House, Wykey, Shrewsbury, SY4 1JA
Tel: 01939 261616 Fax: 01939 261606
E-mail: info@quillerbooks.com
Website: www.swanhillbooks.com

Contents

Foreword by
Field Marshal The Lord Bramall KG GCB OBE MC

A s a past President of MCC and a cricket lover all my life, it gives me the greatest pleasure to write a foreword to Jocelyn Galsworthy's second volume dealing with the Game of which she has become so much part.

In her first volume – *White Hats and Cricket Bats* – Jocelyn, with her enchanting and sensitive pastels, and woven into her life as an artist, introduced us to (or in many cases reminded us of) the most splendid cricket grounds in the world, both the famous and the not so famous, and of course, of the matches played on them. In this volume *Lords of Cricket* she continues to chronicle and capture the spirit and ethos of the game by turning her varied talents to portraiture of a number of leading cricket personalities, all of whom, in their own way, have done much to enhance, develop and promote the game.

Each of the portraits, in this case drawings using sepia and terracotta pencils, has an accompanying biography; and it is not surprising that you will find there, amongst many others, outstanding international batsmen such as Sunil Gavaskar, David Gower, Greg Chappell and Matthew Hayden, and Clive Lloyd and Sir Vivian Richards; famous bowlers such as Sir Richard Hadlee, Fred Trueman, and the record breaker Shane Warne; and the great all rounder, Ian Botham, together with the redoubtable wicket keeper/batsman Adam Gilchrist. Also included are a number of distinguished Test and County cricket captains, including the present and most successful captain of England, Michael Vaughan. But you will also find, and this is what makes the book so fascinating, portraits of others who, in different perhaps less obvious but no less important ways, have helped to make the game what it is. This includes patrons, administrators, cricket writers and broadcasters, umpires and scorers and a groundsman, and a spectator steward, all of whom have contributed much to our enjoyment of cricket.

For an artist to be equally proficient and skillful at portraiture and landscape, and to be able to master more than one medium – in Jocelyn's case charcoal, sepia and terracotta drawing, oils and pastels, shows remarkable accomplishment. When at the same time you are able to use this talent not only to invoke countless happy memories for both players and spectators of cricket, but also to enhance the bibliography of the game, it represents a real achievement

This new volume will, I know, prove a worthy successor to the last one and I commend it to all cricket enthusiast.

Foreword by
The Hon. John Howard, MP, Prime Minister of Australia

Cricket is multi-faceted, involving not only players, but officials, commentators, the media and those who follow the game closely, and support it in various capacities

Jocelyn Galsworthy's initiative therefore to gather together the portraits of a wide cross-section of people who are either involved in the sport or maintain an avid interest in it is to be highly commended and makes the project a particularly exciting one. The more so, given that all those who have agreed to be involved have contributed significantly, in one way or another, to the development and popularity of the game in recent decades.

I note that the proceeds from the sale of the portraits will benefit the Arundel Cricket Foundation in England and the Les Favell Foundation in Australia. Both foundations, of course, aim to provide support to enable those who might not otherwise have the opportunity to play the game to do so and to realise their potential and talent.

As one who enjoys the cricket immensely, I trust the book adds greatly to the appreciation and pleasure that others derive from the game.

(John Howard)

Acknowledgements

I would like to thank all those cricketers, past and present, as well as the TMS team, those at Lord's who appear in the book, His Grace the Duke of Richmond, Christopher Bazalgette, John Woodcock, Sir Ron Brierley and Sir Michael Stoute for their enormous patience in answering my questions and talking about themselves (for most, I imagine, their least favourite subject.) I particularly thank John Woodcock for his help and also Christopher Bazalgette for always being at the other end of the telephone with his computer-like brain ready to snap into action. Jocelyn Galsworthy, too, was a mine of information whenever I was stuck. Anthea Heslop and David Burden deserve thanks for the many times they pulled me up on technicalities and pointed me in the right direction, as does Charlotte Hofton for interviewing Michael Vaughan for me. A great big vote of thanks must go to my long-suffering husband, Robin, with apologies for the many scratch meals and unreasonably late nights. He had a lovely little hut (rather like a cricket pavilion) built for me to work in, away from the house at the bottom of the garden. It was a godsend. I thoroughly recommend the arrangement to all authors.

Jocelyn would like to thank all those who sat patiently for her in England and Australia. They will be pleased to know that the portraits have been widely acclaimed. Terry Davies had the idea which sparked the whole thing off and has been a marvellous help throughout. Thanks go to Philip de Bay for his superb photography of Jocelyn's portraits and to Stephen Sidders of Reliant Colour Solutions for his calmness and attention to detail. Ann Underwood deserves a special mention for coming to the rescue with her excellent secretarial skills – we could not have done without her.

Judy Vigors

Bibliography

Cricket's Great Entertainers, Henry Blofeld, published by Hodder & Stoughton, 2003

A Thirst for Life, Henry Blofeld, published by Hodder & Stoughton, 2000

White Lightning, Allan Donald, published by Collins Willow (Harper Collins), 1999

Gower, David Gower published by Collins Willow (Harper Collins), 1992

As it Was, Memoirs of Fred Trueman, published by Macmillan, 2004

Summers Will Never be the Same, Christopher Martin-Jenkins and Pat Gibson, published by Transworld Publishers Ltd, 1994

The Spirit of Cricket – A personal Anthology, Christopher Martin-Jenkins, published by Faber & Faber Ltd, 1994

A Lot of Hard Yakka, Simon Hughes, published by Headline, 1997

The Cricketer, *Cricketer International* and *The Wisden Cricketer*

Introduction

I was surprised to have been asked by Jocelyn Galsworthy to write brief, light hearted biographies to accompany her marvellously accurate portraits of cricketers past and present, as well as administrators, cricket writers and all the other facets of the diamond which is the game of cricket. I was certainly not an obvious choice.

Having been brought up with the menfolk of my family playing cricket, talking cricket and in later years, viewing cricket on an old black and white television as well as watching the real thing, be it at Test, County or Village level, I confess I ought to have known far more about the game than I do. My mother and I rather shut ourselves away when the talk was of cricket, only putting in an appearance in order to feed and water these armchair sportsmen. I have the impression that football has much the same effect on the majority of the female population today.

As part of the *Lords of Cricket* project, I was taken to Adelaide where I met and interviewed cricketers of the calibre of Clive Lloyd, Mark Taylor, Sunil Gavaskar, Greg Chappell, Matthew Hayden and Darren Lehmann. They were so forthcoming, in a modest way, so charming and so enthusiastic about what we were doing that I was completely won over and started to wonder what it was about a game which produced such consistently sterling characters. As my research progressed, I realised I was merely skimming the surface of a sport which had been in existence for many hundred years, evolving over time, but whose basic principles of 'a cool head and a brave heart' as well as a 'quick eye and a nimble body' have not changed and never will.

As a grandmother (of American children, sadly unlikely to play cricket), it is an irony that this maddening and absorbing game now holds me fast in its coils, compelling me to learn more at the very age when the grey cells have begun to diminish along with the eyesight. Happily, I can still make out all those gorgeous young men in their whites and still have the wit to realise what heroes they are. The skill of batsmen like Adam Gilchrist and Andrew Strauss or bowlers like Muttiah Muralitharan and Shane Warne is awesome and the ebb and flow of a Test match almost as much a test for the nerves of the spectators as it is for the players.

Every single portrait in *Lords of Cricket* has been drawn from life and bears the original signature of the sitter, and I have managed to interview personally most of the characters in the book. While Jocelyn drew them, I chatted, asking questions of some, merely listening to others. Of necessity, I have had to rely heavily on autobiographies and memoirs for those I was unable to talk to in person. All writers go to a source for their material, so I make no apology for having to do likewise. The whole point of these short biographies is to try to show the reader the personality of the individual as well as cataloguing, to some extent, their achievements. Some people are household names and legends in their own lifetime and it is extremely presumptuous of me to think I can reveal a side to them hitherto unknown. Cricket has been written about more than any other sport, so if the enthusiasm of the reader for the written word starts to flag, I am hopeful that Jocelyn's brilliant drawings will, nevertheless, prove an enduring source of pleasure to all those who love the noble game.

Judy Vigors
Bembridge, Isle of Wight
April, 2005

Cricket at Goodwood, 300 years 1702-2002
from an oil painting by Jocelyn Galsworthy

THE DUKE

The Duke of Richmond and Gordon

On 2nd November, 1989, the present Duke of Richmond, born 19th September, 1929, succeeded to the Dukedoms of Richmond (England), Lennox (Scotland), Gordon (United Kingdom) and Aubigny (France). He is the tenth Duke to bear the title and to inhabit the ancestral seat at Goodwood in Sussex. The Duke's forbear, Charles II started the whole thing off by begetting the first of the line at Euston Hall, Thetford, on a night between two days' racing at Newmarket. Louise de Keroualle, the lady in question, came from an aristocratic Breton family and served as Maid of Honour to Minette, Charles' beloved sister, married to Monsieur, brother of the French King Louis XIV. Louise came with Minette on a diplomatic visit to England and Charles noticed her. When his sister died soon after, he invited her to come to the English court as Maid of Honour to his Queen, Catherine of Braganza. Louis XIV was only too delighted to let her go, as he thought he would have a ready source of information and influence at the heart of Charles' court. Louise held out for a year before succumbing to the legendary Stuart charm and shortly afterwards he made her Duchess of Portsmouth. There was much rivalry between the French and English mistresses. On one famous occasion, when Nell Gwyn was riding in a closed carriage, the mob mistook her for the catholic Louise de Keroualle, or Madam Carwell as they called her, being unable to get their tongues round her French name. They started shouting and Nell at once stuck her head out of the window and begged the good people to desist because she was the protestant whore! They cheered her loudly for that. Charles loved Louise for the rest of his life and passed his royal title of Duke of Richmond to her son, Charles Lennox.

Life in the 21st century is not quite so colourful, but the Duke and his son, the Earl of March, have given the public plenty of excitement in the form of horseracing at Goodwood, the racecourse high up on the Sussex Downs which he owns. Every year he hosts 'Glorious Goodwood' at the height of the summer. This comprises five days of superb racing in an unrivalled setting, for which only the adjective 'glorious' will do. There are many more meetings throughout the summer and for a large number of racegoers, Goodwood is their favourite course, so much so that His Grace receives dozens of requests for people to have their ashes scattered there, when the time comes. It has changed a bit since Edward VII and Lily Langtry used to stay for the races and now boasts several excellent restaurants, all the usual facilities and a shop selling beautifully-produced items with the Goodwood label. All this is the brainchild of the Earl of March, very much approved of by his father and the general public, who consider it a privilege to race there

If the Duke's colours of scarlet and yellow seem familiar to members of MCC, then that is because, according to him, they were offered to the great cricketing establishment, who have adopted them. Cricket was recorded for the first time, at Goodwood in 1702. There is a receipt in existence which shows the purchase of a barrel of brandy to reward the winning team. It seems that eighteenth century cricketers were just as fond of their drink as they are now, only more so. In 1727, the then Duke played two matches against Lord Middleton's Eleven at Peper Harrow and the rules, which the Duke wrote down, were formulated at that time. No-one was allowed to voice an opinion on any point of the game, but Clause 13 stated that this did not apply to the Duke of Richmond. The present Duke decided to commemorate the 300th anniversary of cricket at Goodwood by staging a three-match festival, beginning on August 30th 2002 with a match between the Duke of Richmond's Eleven and the Lord's Taverners. The next game was to be played by the Duke's Eleven against Hambledon in eighteenth century costume, using the rules drawn up by the second Duke in 1727. The third day saw an MCC Team, captained by the evergreen Colin Ingleby-MacKenzie take the field against the Duke's Eleven. The second Duke's rules were also given an airing in 1977, on the occasion of the 250th anniversary of the Peper Harrow match. The Duke, himself, was the wicketkeeper and was amazed to see the ball (which had been bowled underarm) pass through the middle of the wicket without dislodging the only bail. In those days, there were only two stumps and since you were not out unless the bail fell off, the third stump was introduced to prevent the ball from passing through. There were, of course, no pads or gloves and the scorer kept tally by cutting a notch in a stick with a knife. Peter Graves, an Oxford Blue, who played for Sussex, fielded at cover and threw the ball so hard at the gloveless wicketkeeper, that he couldn't write for a week afterwards. Next time, he would make sure he umpired instead, in a full-skirted frock coat, wig and three-cornered hat.

Originally, if you played cricket for Goodwood club, you were almost certainly in the employ of the second

Duke. It is said he chose his servants on their cricketing merits, so fond was he of the game. Ostensibly, they were gardeners and coachmen but their real purpose was to play cricket. The third Duke had a groom who was a good, fast bowler but knew nothing about horses. The catchment area for club members is not, in these days, the workforce on the Estate, but local people from a ten mile radius. Most of their games are against local villages and clubs, although they also play the Grannies – London, New Zealand and Sussex over-50s. The longest serving player is Peter Willmer, who has been playing for Goodwood since 1961. The ground is available for hire on Saturdays and mid-week and the revenue has helped bring about improvements such as electricity to the pavilion, enabling the club to set up a much-needed bar, new sight screens ordered from the local blacksmith, an artificial net, a new scoreboard, a three ton roller and roll-on, roll-off covers. There has also been substantial improvement to the surface which used to be slow and flat and is now speedier and bouncier, thanks to the introduction of clay-based loam.

Sadly, the Earl of March has hardly played cricket since leaving Eton, being much more interested in motor sports. Once a year, he holds a Festival of Speed at Goodwood House, bringing together any and everyone who is interested in old and not so old, racing cars. Many celebrities from the racing world come along and it is always an exciting and nostalgic occasion to see such wonderful cars lined up in front of Goodwood House. His grandfather, the 9th Duke had been a motor-racing driver in the Brooklands era and founded the Goodwood Motor Circuit on his estate in Sussex.

The Duke's grandmother used to play cricket at Goodwood in the twenties, and belonged to 'The White Heather Ladies' who frequently found themselves playing against boys' prep schools. The Duke went to Ludgrove under the present headmaster, Gerald Barber's grandfather. He played cricket there, but was sent to America in 1940, where he played baseball instead and at school in Princeton, New Jersey, played soccer but not cricket. He returned to England at the age of 14. He maintains that he was the sort of chap you sent in to open the innings and keep things quiet while the others got runs. Every year, as a young man, he would bring a team of friends down to play at Goodwood. There was always a lunch beforehand and on one of these occasions the Duke discovered some bottles of a Russian liqueur in the Goodwood cellar, which had been presented by the Tzar of Russia when he visited in 1902. He gave the teams a goodly amount of this firewater and found that the fast bowlers were able to bowl two fast overs before collapsing in a heap, having to be carried off the field. The Duke's wicket-keeping was brought to an end when his cheekbone was broken by an extremely fast ball, which the batsman hit backwards. He spent nine days in Chichester hospital on the strength of it.

The Duke served in the Territorial Army between 1949 and 1954. He married early, Monica Grenville-Grey at the age of twenty-two and has four daughters and one son. He is a most charming and approachable man, who is so modest and unstuffy at times that it is easy to forget his rank. He would probably say that he is used to it and that it is merely a sign of the times. On one occasion, one of his daughters went into her bank in Chichester to cash a cheque. The staff were new and did not recognise her. She was asked to produce identification which she hadn't brought with her. Result: no cash, although her name was printed on the cheque. Strangely enough, it is the French who make most fuss of the connection between the Duke of Richmond and the monarchy. Louise de Keroualle was given the title Duchesse d'Aubigny, and the Mayor of this 'Ville des Stuarts' invited the present Duke and his family to visit. His youngest daughter wore Louise's ring and they paraded round the town on a royal walkabout to the delight of the populace. The French being huge snobs, thoroughly appreciated this piece of theatre! This Duke has worked most of his life, becoming a chartered accountant and working in the financial controller's department, Courtaulds Ltd. He has been a member of various important Church of England Committees, Organisations and Commissions including the General Synod/Church Assembly as well as a Chancellor of Sussex University, President of several societies, such as the British Horse Society, South East England Tourist Board and Sussex County Cricket Club, African Medical and Research Foundation and on the Board of innumerable companies. The Duke also holds the Medal of Honour, British Equestrian Federation, 1983. He took his seat in the House of Lords as a Cross-Bencher in 1990.

The Duke of Richmond acknowledges how privileged he is, as a Duke and a landowner to be able to take the initiative in so many areas. He has led a full and useful life, as had his younger brother, Lord Nicholas Gordon Lennox, linguist and distinguished diplomat, who died in 2004. He has done, and is doing, a magnificent job, together with the Earl of March of making his great Estate pay its way and of preserving his wonderful heritage while at the same time, allowing us access to his house, his land and his life. He says, ruefully, that his son claims never to have played anything at Eton, but is heartened by the fact that his grandson, at nine, shows great promise. He would like to think that there will be someone to take an interest in his cricket club and keep up the old traditions, though what will happen when the firewater runs out is anyone's guess.

PAST MASTERS

Ian Terence Botham OBE

Ian 'Beefy' Botham, one of the greatest all-rounders to play the game of cricket seems to be as active and energetic at the age of 49, as ever he was. Weighing in at 10 lbs. 1 oz. at birth on 24th November, 1955, he announced to the world that he was going to be no pushover. He demonstrated his fearlessness and energy at a very young age when still in his playpen (and dying to get out). He refused to be left on his own and materialised at his mother's feet in another room, not once but every time she returned him to the safety of his playpen. More than a little puzzled, she watched unseen while baby Botham lifted up a corner of his prison, balanced it on his toybox, crawled out and replaced the playpen exactly as it had been. This was a lad to keep your eye on, clearly, but easier said than done. Ian was a tearaway, full of spirit and curiosity. No wonder his mother kept a wooden spoon close by to encourage discipline.

Fortunately, sport came to the rescue. He played plenty of cricket and football at school, but somehow always managed to satisfy the academic requirements as well. He started playing in earnest at the tender age of fifteen and a half, when he turned professional. In 1973, he made his one-day debut for Somerset and his Test debut for England at Trent Bridge on 28th July, 1977, against Australia in the third match of the Ashes series. He felt distinctly nervous coming in to bowl for the first time and, because he was trying so hard, achieved nothing. His captain, Mike Brearley, suggested he take a breather and then put him in to bowl again immediately after lunch. That did the trick and the great Greg Chappell was well and truly bowled, much to Ian's amazement and delight. He finished the day with 5 for 74. To cap it all, he was presented to the Queen, who as part of her Silver Jubilee was visiting the ground. According to Ian, there wasn't a hat big enough for him, that day. As time progressed, however, his policy of playing hard on and off the field led to much negative press coverage and, inevitably, wrist-slapping, but the public continued to flock to watch this charismatic, aggressive and exciting player, warts and all. The name, Botham, today commands huge respect in the rest of the world as well as it does at home. It was I. T. Botham who seemed to change the attitude of the England side. He played to win and had self-belief which rubbed off on the rest of the team.

His friendship with the peerless Viv Richards, which began in their Somerset days, has been of the greatest significance to him throughout his life. "Viv Richards", he declares with feeling, "is the greatest player I have ever seen, and in my opinion, he was the best in the world." He is not just saying that because he and Viv were close. They shared a house in Taunton for twelve years, and Viv is godfather to Ian's son, Liam, who plays Rugby League for the Leeds Rhinos. In Ian's words, "he is part of the family." Extremely loyal, when Viv Richards and Joel Garner were sacked from Somerset, Ian went too. Now both Viv Richards and Ian Botham have a permanent presence at the county ground at Taunton, in the shape of the Botham stand and the Richards Gates.

Ian's cricketing career speaks for itself. One has only to look back at the 1981 Ashes series, where he turned round the fortunes of the match at Headingley, in such spectacular fashion that the series became known ever after as 'Botham's Ashes'. The series was commemorated in 2001, twenty years after the event. A plaque was unveiled by Richie Benaud, on the site of a confectionery stall, hit for six by Ian during his amazing innings of 149, not out. The plaque features a picture of the stallholder, one Arthur Hecklethwaite, who swallowed a gobstopper in panic, when he thought the ball was coming straight for him! Those heady days are now gone, but not forgotten and Ian has managed to channel his energies into various new projects, some charitable, some commercial, all of them seemingly successful and he does appear to be completely satisfied with his life as it is today. Sky Sports employ him, under exclusive contract, as a cricket commentator. This is a job he loves and admits that he could not work for a better employer. Sky Sports, he says, is progressive, with coverage of a high standard, enabling people all round the globe to see cricket and other sports, on tap, whenever they want. Apart from the day job, Ian owns jointly with Bob Willis and Geoff Merrill of Australia, a wine label 'BMW'. The company produces a chardonnay, a cabernet and a shiraz, three grape varieties grown in the McLaren Valley and Coonawarra. It has proved to be extremely popular and is stocked in supermarkets, restaurants and hotels. Ian, naturally, has a say in the style of wine made, but since he doesn't ask Geoff Merrill to play cricket, he feels he ought to leave the wine-making to the experts. Ian has acquired a great deal of knowledge about wine, more than likely by drinking as many bottles as possible (he is a generous host) while learning to differentiate and appreciate at the same time. He is, probably, a connoisseur, but is he a wine snob? He could be, but Ian

is about as far removed from snobbery as it is possible to be. He is a completely genuine, down-to-earth man, who needs no BS repellent. He is confident in himself and his abilities, straightforward though not ingenuous, and stands by his opinions, however unpalatable. At a World Cup Final dinner, when the Australians, one hopes in an uncharacteristic moment, chose to make fun of the Queen, Ian walked out in disgust. He is, very definitely, a man's man, whatever the press may print, but someone as outwardly full of machismo as Ian will always attract the opposite sex, and to be fair, he has not discouraged them in the past. The late John Arlott summed it all up when he said "We expect this chap Botham to work cricketing miracles every day and still behave like a sombre vegetable – well, you just can't expect that, the two things just don't go together." The main thing is that Ian owns up to his peccadilloes and regrets the hurt they caused.

He is very fortunate, indeed, to have a wonderful wife in Kath, to whom he has been married for almost thirty years. They have three offspring, two daughters and a son. Their daughter, Sarah, works for BSkyB as floor manager, Becky is a beautician and Liam, a Rugby player. He also has grandchildren (as seen on television, advertising breakfast cereal), who call him 'Grandad Beefy'. He is inordinately proud of all his family. Children seem to strike a chord with Ian. Some years ago, he was moved unbearably at the sight of small children dying of leukaemia. He wanted to help in any way he could and hit upon the idea of raising funds by walking. In his last great walk – having undertaken 14 altogether – he marched from John o' Groats to Land's End in just 34 days, helping to swell his fundraising efforts to a staggering £4.5 million. He pays particular tribute to Matthew Maynard, who ran up and down tirelessly with a tin (or was it a bucket?) collecting the public's pounds and pennies.

Since retiring from the game, Ian has no desire at all to play cricket, but he does play golf rather well and has now become an intrepid skier, regularly taking his grandchildren on skiing holidays, "where", he complains with a twinkle, "they ski past me all the time". He is being modest, as his avowed aim, one of three he still has left in life, is to someday beat the Austrian superstar of the piste, Franz Klammer (a personal friend), in a downhill run. With Beefy you never know, he could do it. Aim number two is to win the Dunhill Links with Ian Woosnam (after which there will be two woozy Ians) and catch a 40lb salmon – not all on the same day, though. Ian seems a man happy in his own skin, content with life but not complacent. He acknowledges that he played cricket in the right era for him. Although playing the West Indies in their heady days was an extremely intense experience, it was always fun. The players of the present age are pampered in a way unthinkable in his day, but he would not have wanted it otherwise. Life has been good to him; he lives in a beautiful house in his favourite part of the world within a loving family framework, and he would not wish to change any of it. He travels all over the world, doing a job which suits him down to the ground. What could be better than that?

Ian Terence Botham
b. 24th November, 1955 Heswall, Cheshire, England
Right hand bat
Right arm fast medium
O.B.E. 1992 for services to cricket and charity
Laureus Academy Member
BBC Personality of the Year Lifetime Achievement Award 2004

David Ivon Gower OBE

David Gower first saw the light of day in respectable Tunbridge Wells, where his grandmother lived. His mother had been born in Mombasa and his father worked in Tanganyika (as the country was then known), and they were home on leave when David was born. Six months later, he was taken back to Africa where he remained until he was six. His father, who had been a Cambridge hockey Blue, was a member of the Gymkhana Club in Dar es Salaam, and a good all-rounder. An early photograph shows David with a cricket bat at the Gymkhana Club and as he grew up, although he played various sports, cricket edged ahead. The family returned to England where his father got a job at what is, nowadays, Loughborough University, and David had the run of the excellent sports facilities during the holidays. He went to school at Marlborough House, Kent and was awarded a scholarship to King's Canterbury – his father's old school – from where he gained a place at University College, London, reading Law. By the time he was at University, he was already playing professional cricket and his heart was simply not in his Law degree. He lasted only a year, despite warnings that he should not think of relying on sport to make a living. He went straight from his last exam at UCL to playing in a Benson and Hedges quarter final for Leicestershire. In 1975, Leicestershire won their first county championship and the Benson and Hedges Cup.

As David's career progressed, he realised that although good things were predicted for him, he was still at the very beginning and had a great deal to learn. Fortunately, he had Ray Illingworth as his captain and a very experienced squad, some of whom were more than willing to pass on their knowledge. Illy became his mentor and his three or four years under him proved to be a very good grounding for life as a professional cricketer. It is all quite different now and the players expect money, cars and all the trappings before they have proved themselves. David started out at £25 a week (and was thrilled with that) and an ancient Ford Anglia, which his mother had driven in Dar es Salaam. Having survived the dirt tracks of Tanganyika and been carefully maintained for eleven years, it took a mere three months before David put it into a hedge. He subsequently bought a heap from the groundsman, which blew up. At that stage, he was playing cricket for fun – the better he played the more fun it became and he progressed smoothly upward, hardly noticing how far he had come

and the reputation he was starting to acquire. Here was this elegant batsman with blonde, curly hair and angelic looks, who was capable of brilliant strokes but who exasperated the crowd and the hierarchy by throwing away his advantage with ill-considered shots. However, he was described by one commentator as 'a caresser in an era of biffers', a remark which attested to his graceful and stylish use of the bat.

He has been accused of being too 'laid-back', not competitive or ambitious enough and of not taking the game seriously. He refutes all of these charges. As someone who does not wear his heart on his sleeve or believe in being grim and earnest all the time, he was often misunderstood. He was certainly ambitious in that he wanted, very much, to play for England and to do the best job he could for his county as well as his country. Perhaps he had not quite grown up and did not take everything as seriously as he should, but his good brain and sense of the absurd refused, at times, to be squashed by rules and regulations designed to enforce uniformity. David was an individual with a curious mind-set. He found too much net-practice and too little humour stultifying and felt he simply had to relieve the tedium somehow. In 1973, his father sadly died and David felt his loss keenly. When he scored his maiden first-class century in 1976 playing against Middlesex at Lord's, he wished his father had been there to see it. He would have been so proud. He was bowled for a duck in the first innings, hardly a promising beginning, but the second innings saw him make a relaxed century. In typical fashion, he had spent lunch asleep as he had been out the night before, until dawn. In 1977, it was rumoured that he would be picked for the England side, but Mike Gatting was chosen instead. David toured the Far East that year and a friendship with Chris Cowdrey developed. He played plenty of good cricket and ended up in Perth, playing club cricket for the rest of the winter. The following season he joined the England side for the one-day matches against Pakistan, scoring a century in the second of the two games. His Test debut came hot on the heels of the one-dayers, at Edgbaston against Pakistan, where the very first ball he hit off the bowling of left-arm seamer Liaquat Ali (known as Liquid), went for four runs. He averaged 51 for the series against Pakistan, under the captaincy of Mike Brearley. His first Test century came against New Zealand at the Oval and his average for the series this time was 57. Add to that his score of 1000 runs

in a season for the first time and it looked as though his promise was being fulfilled.

He writes, in his excellent autobiography, of the special feeling about the Test Match dressing room encountered for the very first time. Just looking at the Team Sheet and seeing his name alongside the greats of the game gave him a tremendous buzz. The bigger the occasion, the better David seemed to perform and the opportunity to shine on the international stage soon presented itself. In 1978/9, David toured Australia with the England Team and they won the series 5-1, the first time an England team had won five Tests in any series. David made his first overseas Test century at Perth and headed the England averages with 42. He was to tour Australia many times and grow to love the country, which corresponded exactly to his lifestyle. Dennis Lillee and David Gower, Test bowler and Test batsman, greatly respected and admired one another, a fact which fills him with pride. The Chappell brothers got to know him and he liked them and appreciated their advice. The Australians, although facing 'the old enemy' on the field, were the first to be hospitable off it.

David's nickname of 'Lubo' was coined in Adelaide when he visited an eaterie of the same name, and it stuck. Lubo's famous prank with a Tiger Moth – buzzing the cricket pitch when the game was still in progress – took place at Carrara, Queensland's answer to Las Vegas, and has entered the annals of cricket lore. What got into him? Boredom? A rush of blood to the head? It was funny at the time, but the authorities were not amused. Poor Lubo (or should it have been Lupy?) was thoroughly dressed down along with John Morris and fined £1000. The Australians thought that the whole incident was a storm in a teacup, but the England selectors did not. In the summer of 1992, he returned to Hampshire (for whom he played after leaving Leicestershire), hoping to regain his place in the England side. But it was not to be and David Gower, the hugely entertaining, hugely talented left-hand batsman bowed out for good. There was a terrific outcry from players and public alike as well as many tributes to his stylish and very individual contribution to English cricket. It is significant that many people – players and knowledgeable observers – rate him as the most enthralling batsman ever to watch. As captain both of his county, Leicestershire and his country, he distinguished himself many times, regaining the Ashes in 1985, when the England team produced batting of the highest order and completely dominated the Australian bowlers. The same year, Leicestershire won the Benson & Hedges Cup.

But David is nothing if not canny where he and his finances are concerned. He had been writing for The Times as well as broadcasting and doing television for Channel 9 and Sky, long before he gave up playing cricket. All the right options were already in place and his wonderful agent, Jon Holmes, who handled Peter Shilton and Gary Lineker as well as David, would be brokering deals all the time so that he built for his clients a career after sport, into which they could slot without any hiatus. David's core job is for Sky Sports, and very good he is at it, too. In Cape Town recently, he interviewed Archbishop Desmond Tutu, who had come along to watch the cricket. He struck exactly the right note with the much loved cleric, neither condescending nor too searching, patiently listening with interest to what he had to say and there is no doubt that the interviewer got the best out of his interviewee to everyone's satisfaction.

He writes for the *Sunday Times* but does not feel he has a flair for the written word. He enjoys his appearances on television, even, occasionally, on the show 'They think it's all Over', which it is, as he no longer does it. While he was captain and the last to know, a tour to South Africa was mooted and many players signed up because of the amount of money they were being offered. David was advised against doing so, as it would jeopardise his future earning power. He took the warning seriously. He did very well out of his benefit year and invested wisely. The result is that David has an extremely comfortable lifestyle with his wife, Thorunn and two daughters, Alex and Sammi. He collects art, mainly wildlife and if the press is to be believed, always has a case of Bollinger on hand, probably ready chilled. He is still a very attractive man, although the blonde hair is turning to silver and, apart from a few niggling ailments, mostly muscular or skeletal, he seems to be in good shape. He plays tennis and golf, but his main interest lies in helping preserve and protect African wildlife. This interest took off as the result of an impulse buy of a print of cheetahs by David Shepherd, the prominent wildlife artist (not to be confused with the eminent umpire of the same name). When, later, he met the artist, he was asked to join the David Shepherd Conservation Foundation as a Board member, raising money for endangered species. When Lubo decides to go on safari, he does it with style, naturally. He spent a fabulous nine days with four course dinners and chilled Bollinger every night, in the middle of nowhere. It was heaven.

Unforgettably brilliant and exasperating at the same time, humorous, stylish and graceful, (one feels that if Sir Percy Blakeney ever played the noble game, he would have done so like Gower), with sudden lapses in expected behaviour, David clashed with authority on many occasions. His best friends in the England side were Lamby and 'Both', the only trouble there being that he could not keep up with them after dark! He made cricket seem easy and fun and kept everyone entertained which, after all, is half the purpose of professional cricket. He won many awards, but the one he cherishes most is a spurious accolade from a national newspaper. It reads 'For Fun and Excellence' (and might have added 'in the face of adversity'). These words encapsulate the philosophy by which David lives and, he reckons, would make a thoroughly fitting epitaph when the time comes.

David Ivon Gower
b. 1st April, 1957 Tunbridge Wells, Kent, England
Left hand bat
Right arm off break
Commentator

Clive Hubert Lloyd CBE

Clive Lloyd is an imposing man by any standards. The statistics have it that he is 6'5" tall, with stooping shoulders, a large moustache and thick glasses. What the statistics fail to mention is that he is a most courteous and affable man who speaks softly and is very modest about his achievements, which are legion.

Born on 31st August, 1944 in Georgetown, Demerara, British Guiana, Clive was surrounded by the sort of influences which would guarantee a love of cricket. He grew up with his cousin, Lance Gibbs as his inspiration and he would play for hours in their two back yards – one for batting and one for bowling. Lance Gibbs became a spin-bowling legend who took 309 Test wickets while Clive, the younger by ten years, became one of the most successful captains ever and the king-pin of the operation which saw the rise of the West Indies to the very top of world cricket where they dominated for many years.

Clive remembers that, as a child, he had to be inventive since nothing was handed to him on a plate. A jockey had given his father a balata whip made of thick rubber, which to Clive seemed just the job for a homemade cricket ball. He boiled the whip to the right consistency, then using the hollow at the bottom of a brandy bottle, he moulded the rubber into a ball with which he and his friends could play. He liked to practice at the Demerara Cricket Club in the holidays when no one was about. To this end, he and his friends bribed the caretaker with a half-bottle of rum to make him sleepy so that they could play undisturbed.

Clive made his Test debut as a left-handed batsman against India in December 1966, hitting 82 not out and gained his first Test century in Trinidad against England. By the fourth Test of that series he had added another 100 to confirm his arrival on the world-class scene. In 1968-69, touring Australia he notched up a further Test century at Brisbane. He signed for Lancashire and made his debut for the Manchester club in 1968. At that match, the Australian umpire Cec Pepper asked how he bowled, left or right and then called out, "batsman, there's a change of bowler and a change of colour!" He was a powerful, hard-hitting batsman who, when on song, could notch up runs very fast – he once scored a double century against Glamorgan in 120 minutes equalling the record for the quickest first-class double hundred. As a right-arm medium pace bowler he took 114 first-class wickets in all, including ten Test wickets. He was also the first West Indian player to earn 100 international caps. But it is for his brilliant captaincy of the West Indies that he will be best remembered. He was responsible for the longest run of success which any team has known in international cricket. He moulded a group of individuals, all highly talented but lacking cohesion, into a formidable, united team. He commanded respect from his players because he was willing to stand by them and fight for better pay and conditions and for recognition of their ability. He gave them pride in themselves and pride in being a team with the belief that they could win matches. Add to this his formidable array of bowlers and it is little wonder that his captaincy was so effective. In his foreword to Michael Manley's book, *A History of West Indies Cricket*, published in 1988, Clive writes about cricket being the ethos around which West Indian society revolves with cricket being the instrument of Caribbean cohesion. He acknowledges a debt to the great Sir Frank Worrall, whom he tried to emulate in his leadership of the West Indies. It is all rather different now, however, and Clive must be saddened to see the decline in fortunes of the side he once captained to greatness. In fact, Clive bemoans the all round decline in standards of behaviour and respect for officials as witnessed in South Africa recently. As the senior match referee, his task seems to be getting harder. The umpires complain of the same thing and not without justification. Consider the death threats to Steve Bucknor and Aleem Dar. That the captain of England should question the umpires' decision in the 'Lightmetergate' affair and call for more consistency on the part of the officials, shows a distinct lack of respect, Clive maintains. The fact that he, himself, commented on a confidential disciplinary hearing has seen him, too, receive a rap over the knuckles. It must all seem very perplexing to one who has had such an outstanding career. In spite of this contretemps (not the first and certainly not the last), Clive Lloyd is a highly respected ICC match referee, a job for which a man of his calibre must, surely, be eminently suited.

Clive has won many awards over the years, beginning with *Wisden* Cricketer of the Year in 1971 for his outstanding contribution to Lancashire over the previous year, scoring 1600 runs for the county. He was Man of the Match five times and in 1993 was awarded a CBE. He has a son who was chosen to play for England in the under-15 World Cup and who now plays basketball for The Melbourne Tigers and cricket for Prahran. All this despite contracting a serious illness as an infant, it is thought from having the MMR vaccination. As Clive puts it, "he was one of the lucky ones". Since Clive himself was a schoolboy

athletics champion, he must be pleased, though not altogether surprised that his son is a chip off the old block.

Although Clive has lived in England, in Lancashire near Old Trafford for thirty years and brought up his children in the county, he has a certain fondness for Australia where the climate is very much to his liking. Will he retire there? Perhaps, but certainly not in the immediate future and not while there are Test matches which need his guiding hand.

Clive Hubert Lloyd CBE
b. 31st August 1944, Georgetown, Demerara, British Guiana
Left hand bat
Right arm medium
ICC Match Referee

Gregory Stephen Chappell MBE

Greg Chappell is yet another famous son of Adelaide, South Australia. He was born on 7th August 1948 and right from the start he was surrounded by, and encouraged to, love the game of cricket.

His grandfather, Victor Richardson, had captained Australia in five Tests and his father, who loved cricket and baseball equally, saw to it that Greg and his brothers played at every opportunity. He and a family friend coached them and they spent many long hours in their back yard or in the local park and on the beach, batting and bowling to each other.

Greg recalls seeing the great Ray Lindwall at the end of his career playing in a Test match at the Adelaide Oval. When the match was over, Greg rushed to the nearest park and practised the Lindwall run-up and action. He admitted he and his brothers were not trained for much else, so it came as no surprise when he took up the game professionally. His brother Ian had represented South Australia at the age of 18 and Greg was encouraged by this. If he can do it, I can do it, was his attitude.

Greg was educated at Prince Albert College, Adelaide where there was a good cricket coach, and then went straight from school into District Club cricket. By the following October he, too, was representing South Australia. It took some years for him to be picked for the Australian Team. In late 1968/69 Greg played for Somerset, where he not only batted but fielded brilliantly at slip and used his medium pace bowling to good advantage. His Test debut came in 1970/71 in Perth against Ray Illingworth's England side. He made a century which, he says, was a bit of a wake-up call for his brother Ian, giving him the incentive to make sure he had a permanent place in the team.

It is acknowledged that Greg Chappell was the outstanding Australian batsman of his generation. A tall, elegant cricketer with an upright, somewhat unbending stance, his strength lay largely in his timing and concentration. He batted with authority, and his calmness was used to good effect to discomfit the bowlers.

He became captain of Australia after his brother Ian, and managed to make a century in each innings of his debut as captain, a feat which has never been equalled. He also passed Donald Bradman's aggregate with 7110 runs in Test cricket.

Greg loved playing in the West Indies. In the 1973 Test in Jamaica the crowds and their activities, the music and the colour all enthralled him. He noticed, and was amused by, all the people up in the trees outside the ground getting a free view of the proceedings. On one occasion Uton Dowe, the much-vaunted fast bowler, began his stint with 'Stacky' (Keith Stackpole) on strike, who was looking forward to facing him. Uton bowled too many short balls and when Rohan Kanhai, the West Indies captain, took him off, someone in the crowd shouted the eleventh commandment "Dowe shall not bowl!" This was typical of West Indian humour and Greg loved it. He also loved going to England, which he felt was the ultimate test. According to Greg, his best innings came when he played at Lord's in 1972, his first Test Match there, dominated by the bowlers.

No account of Greg's career would be complete without the infamous underarm incident in New Zealand, when he ordered his younger brother Trevor to bowl underarm to prevent New Zealand from getting the six they needed for a draw. This was a complete aberration on his part as captain, for which he takes full responsibility. He states now that he was probably mentally unfit to be captain of Australia at that time. However, the attitude of the New Zealanders was extremely generous, and Greg was told by Geoff Howarth, his New Zealand counterpart, to put it all behind him and get on with the game. It still sticks in his mind and still rankles with him.

Since retiring in 1984, Greg has had an iron in many fires. He has run several businesses, some less successful than others, been in financial services, coached the South Australian Redbacks and served on the Australian Cricket Board until 1988. He was State Manager of Cricket in South Australia, responsible for cricketers from an early age through to the under 19s. He is a commentator on Channel 9 alongside his brother Ian (who writes for the *Daily Telegraph*), Richie Benaud, Bill Lawry and Tony Greig.

In 1993 Greg became a committed vegetarian when he joined his wife Judy on a 40-day 'cleansing diet'. He says he has never looked back. He now promotes this way of life through books, including veganism for pets, and has written a controversial treatise on men's health.

Early in 2000, to help celebrate the new millennium, Greg was named in the ACB's Team of the Century. To be chosen as one of the 12 best cricketers of the past century is a great honour. Standing on stage with his boyhood idols, knowing that he was deemed worthy to have a place among the greats of Australian cricket, was a truly emotional moment for him and one he will never forget.

In 2002 Greg Chappell entered the Australian Cricket Hall of Fame and he and his brother Ian now have a permanent memorial in the new Chappell Stands at the beautiful Adelaide Oval.

Greg Stephen Chappell
b. 7th August 1948, Adelaide, South Australia
Right-hand bat
Right arm medium pace leg-break
Slip fielder

Sir Isaac Vivian Alexander Richards KGN OBE

Sir Viv Richards believes in mental strength. He believes in showing real passion for the game of cricket and for giving it your all. Just by looking into someone's eyes, he can see whether there is steely determination to win or not. In Sir Viv's day, none of the bowlers who faced him could possibly have doubted that he meant business. There was hardly a bowler who did not feel a queasy knot in the pit of his stomach when this lithe, powerful figure sauntered to the crease, brimming with self confidence, to take guard. Although chewing the cud incessantly, he was about as bovine as a proud Pamplona bull, snorting and pawing the ground, itching to toss the impertinent matador over his head. There have been very few batsmen in the history of the game who have been able to dismiss the likes of Lillee, Willis and Thomson with such apparent ease and enjoyment. Viv never even wore a helmet, and that in itself intimidated the bowlers by calling their bluff. Once, when he was hit on the jaw by a ball deliberately bowled to inflict damage, he merely massaged the sore spot for a bit. Realising that the bowler would try this trick again, he was waiting for it and contemptuously hooked it to the boundary, going on to make a century.

Viv Richards was born on the Caribbean island of Antigua, on 7th March, 1952. His first cricket was played on the beaches of his island, on the wet, tightly-packed sand to be found at the water's edge. Bowling was like playing ducks and drakes as the ball would skim through the water before making contact with the bat. The bats were just flat pieces of wood shaped to resemble bats and the boys pretended they were proper cricketers, playing for real. As he grew older, Viv and his friends used to play in rough, uneven fields. When it came to fielding, he instinctively raced to the ball, picking it up in one hand, even though it was bouncing all over the place, while simultaneously flinging it at the wicketkeeper or the stumps. He became fleet-footed and eagle-eyed and his fielding in the slips or in the covers was a joy to behold when later he played for his country and for Somerset. In this way, he developed his own, natural style unhindered by too much formal coaching. In the first World Cup final at Lord's in 1975, he spectacularly ran out three Australians as easily as if he had been back in the rough field of his boyhood. As a young boy, Viv used to daydream about scoring centuries by hitting sixes. He maintains that it is very important to have a vision of success in your mind. The night before a match, he often dreamed of making a century, but never a duck. Fear of failure before he had even gone out to bat never troubled him. Having a belief in himself and a positive mental attitude was all he needed to exude his famous self-confidence, which was often mistaken for arrogance. To play the game well, a cricketer must enjoy it and in the Caribbean they enjoy hitting hard. No-one hits harder than Viv Richards. He was not called 'The Master Blaster' for nothing.

Viv's friendship with another hard-hitter, Ian 'Beefy' Botham, started when they met at Somerset in the early 1970s. Viv wrote in the foreword to Ian's autobiography, 'Say the name Ian Botham to me and the first thought I have is not of 'Beefy' the great cricketer but of a magnificent friend, full of love for people, full of support and ready to give you everything he's got.' They shared a house in Taunton for twelve years and when Ian married and had a son, Viv was asked to be his godfather. It is usually the case that 'birds of a feather flock together', so those qualities Viv sees in Ian are more than likely mirrored in himself. During the late 1970s and early 1980s Somerset had enjoyed a level of success they could only have dreamed of. The two West Indians Viv Richards and Joel Garner made up a large part of this success with their brilliance. It seemed impossible that two of the brightest stars in Somerset's firmament could be asked to leave, but that is exactly what happened. Ian was playing at the Oval when Viv telephoned to tell him the news. Without having to think twice, Ian said he was going to leave with them. Viv went on to play for Glamorgan and did them proud by helping them win a Sunday League Trophy. The friendship continues and Viv is now a member of the Botham family, albeit an honorary one. His time is spent nowadays promoting Antigua, attending media events and commentating. One of his passions is making sure that youngsters have the opportunity to play cricket. He has set up the Sir Vivian Richards Foundation expressly for the purpose of encouraging children to develop and express themselves through the game of cricket. It would be very exciting if he found someone like himself when he was just starting out, whom he could help fulfil his potential.

Sir Viv has recently resigned as Chairman of Selectors for the West Indies. There seems to be friction between him and the current captain, Brian Lara. Viv is worried by the attitude of the players and questions their motivation and will to win. There does not seem to be the same level of commitment as before and he lays the blame for this squarely on the captain's shoulders. The players, he

insists, must show real passion for the game. To illustrate the point he says that he used to go to bed with his bat and pads when he played for his country, placing his bat so that it would be the first thing he saw on waking. It worries him, too, that the average height of the fast bowlers has shrunk. "Our quicks" he remembers, "were 6'5" and now they are 5'7!" There is nothing wrong in his eyes, however, with the motivation of the England team under the captaincy of Michael Vaughan. He reckons they are forming into a class outfit. He singles out Freddie Flintoff as being a man who can turn matches and he is particularly pleased to note that, when you look into his eyes, you see the will to win.

Viv still plays cricket for Lashings, and is still as mentally focused as ever, "but", he sighs, "it's not so easy to score runs anymore… the balls look like peas and I can't see 'em and I can't hit 'em". Well, anno domini might have caught up with him but it cannot take away his past glory. Sir Viv made 8,540 runs in 121 Test appearances, with 24 centuries. He once made 100 runs off 56 balls. That was quick. Although he stopped playing first-class cricket more than ten years ago, the old charisma and the attitude are still there for all to see. As a player, as a highly successful captain of the West Indies, never losing a Test series, as a superb county player for Somerset and Glamorgan, as a cricketing legend and supra nova, Sir Vivian Richards has no equal.

The final tribute should be left to his long-time buddy, Botham. "Simply the best of my era and I, personally, find it hard to believe that there has ever been a better batsman. Whatever the conditions, whatever the match-situation, no matter who the opposition or the type of cricket, he was the man you would back to score runs for your life. An intimidating sight at the crease, his refusal ever to wear a batting helmet sent out a clear message: 'I'm not afraid of anyone and I'm certainly not afraid of you'. Watching him smash me and the rest of the England attack for the fastest century of all time in Antigua in 1986 was one of the most extraordinary experiences of my career. That day I felt I was in the presence of greatness. It was like bowling at God."

Sir Isaac Vivian Alexander Richards
b. 7th March, 1952, St. John's, Antigua
Right hand bat
Right arm spin
Slip fielder
Wisden Cricketer of the Year 1977
Knighted in 2000
Inducted into Hartford Hall of Fame 2001

Allan Anthony Donald

The little boy with the blonde hair, born in Bloemfontein, South Africa, Afrikaans-speaking until he was fourteen years old, grew up to be an outstanding representative of the fledgling Rainbow Nation. He was honoured by none other than President Mandela with a special lifetime achievement award for South African sport – one of only six. Allan Donald deserved it and it was all the sweeter coming, as it did, from the hand of the man who together with F. W. de Klerk, had managed to heal the differences between black and white, in so far as was possible, without bloody revolution. Allan's part was to have helped give South Africans pride in their national cricket side. Cricket, being largely the preserve of the white man before Mandela, now represented all the people and Allan had to get used to being shaken by the hand and congratulated when he walked down the street. "At last," he says, "we are being supported because we are South African, irrespective of colour". It was a long time coming and Allan thought he might be better off playing for England, which he was entitled to do, but Ali Bacher convinced him that South Africa was poised to come in from the cold. In 1991 South Africa was readmitted to international sport and Allan Donald was right there to make his contribution. Nicknamed 'White Lightening' (also the title of his autobiography), when he took the field for South Africa against India in Calcutta in 1991/2, their first one-day international since Apartheid, he took five wickets for 29 runs. He shared the Man of the Match award with Sachin Tendulkar and announced in no uncertain terms that he was here to stay. Five months later his international Test career began, against the West Indies at the Kensington Oval Bridgetown, Barbados.

By this time, Allan had been playing for Warwickshire for five years. As a raw recruit he was given a few pointers by Andy Moles on his arrival at Edgbaston, settled in and was taken to a pub, where he had his very first taste of alcohol – aged 21. His parents didn't drink and Bloemfontein wasn't the place to start. He also met Tina there, the girl he married four years later. As one of eight children she knew all about large families and since Allan loves children and the stability a happy marriage can bring, it all worked out rather well. She is his rock and supports him in all he does. He reckons he was a better cricketer because his home-life was so stable. A defining moment came when he met Gladstone Small, a black cricketer who also played for Warwickshire and found himself in the dressing room with him, changing, something which would have been unthinkable in the old South Africa. The fact that he, and nearly everyone else, were so friendly was an eye opener. Geoff Humpage, the Warwickshire wicket-keeper, helped protect Allan when 'politics' got heavy and kept him laughing, which as everybody knows, is the way

to defuse a volatile situation. It was a time to listen and learn. Before the end of his first season with the county, he had a two-year contract and his salary had been more than doubled. In a match at the end of May, 1989, Allan took 7 for 66 and knew he had impressed. He was now a 'proper' fast bowler. He studied a Richard Hadlee video and realised that mental strength and the ability to out-think a batsman was vital if a bowler was going to collect wickets consistently. Devon Malcolm, too, proved a source of inspiration for his marvellous rhythm and ability to glide in instead of thumping in a flat-footed way, which Allan thought he, himself, did. Andy Lloyd, his captain, talked about 'ease and grace', which became his watchwords.

Allan was not pleased at the arrival of Mike Gatting's Rebel Tour to South Africa which finished early and saw much-needed currency go out of the country and into their pockets, when it could have benefited South African cricket. They had a fairly hostile reception; black people demonstrated and refused to serve them in hotels and restaurants. It seemed that it was a recipe for disaster and violent disaster at that. Fortunately, Ali Bacher, realising his mistake in getting the English rebel team to come to South Africa in the first place, cancelled the rest of the tour. Allan went back to Warwickshire, looking forward to the new season and very quickly felt that he was being cold-shouldered in favour of an overseas batsman, Tom Moody. Allan was given the push, but was immediately signed to play for Worcestershire and was looking forward to playing with 'Beefy', who had left Somerset and joined Worcestershire instead. Suddenly, in a curious volte-face, Allan was given a contract with Warwickshire once more and Tom Moody was the one to pack his bags and head for New Road, Worcester. There followed a disappointing season for Allan and he felt the need to get some wickets under his belt, playing in South Africa. It didn't happen right away but little by little what he had learned in England proved to be of great benefit and he was back on track, bowling well again. Gone were the Springboks (too reminiscent of the old regime) to be replaced by Protea, a South African flower. The Test against England under the captaincy of Kepler Wessels was to be a crusade for Allan and Protea. England were not exactly top of the league in international terms, but the South Africans seemed to be obsessed with this Tour and the real possibility of a win. At Lord's on the first day of the first Test, Archbishop Tutu had been refused admittance because he was not wearing a jacket and tie! He had come to bless the team and eventually common sense prevailed and he was allowed in. Thabo Mbeki was there to lend support and in the spirit of the occasion, wanted to show the world that South Africa was back in business. Their win on that occasion gave tremendous pride to all races of the South African people back home.

Between 1996 and 1998, Protea toured Kenya, India, Pakistan and Australia, hosting one-day and Test series at home against India, Zimbabwe, Australia, Sri Lanka and Pakistan. Then off to England for a Test series plus a triangular one-day tournament. Allan took 99 international wickets during the 1996/7 South African season, 41 in Tests, 58 in the one-day matches. He learned a great deal to his advantage from playing India and came away with his skills honed. He learnt more about reverse swing, when to bowl short and what precise length to bowl on flat pitches. He is of the opinion that England ought to play the sub-continent more often, like the Australians, who find it of great benefit, particularly in the case of learning how to play spinners. Allan has had unpleasantness in the form of vitriolic letters and telephone calls, accusing him of being racist. This came about through sledging when Dravid was batting in South Africa. The huge crowds were noisy and the taunts made by the South African side at the Indians did not go down at all well with them. (The Pakistanis, however, seem to give as good as they get). This very aggressive form of sledging is now, if not exactly a thing of the past, becoming less important. The Australians had a cleanup under Mark Taylor and it is very much better nowadays. However, in Allan's case, there was nothing racist about it. He would have said the same to any batsman he was trying to remove, whatever his race.

Allan Donald has had a wonderfully successful cricketing career. As one of Test cricket's very best fast bowlers respected throughout the world, he had a phenomenal strike-rate and was the first South African to take 300 wickets. He took 11 wickets in a one-off Test against Zimbabwe in October, 1995, but was sometimes left out of the one-day team. At the quarterfinal stage of the 1996 World Cup, South Africa, having easily defeated all comers up to that point, were beaten by the West Indies, in the absence of Allan Donald, and bowed out of the competition. The 1999 World Cup semi-final, South Africa v Australia at Edgbaston, was a different matter. Allan still cannot believe how this match slipped through their fingers. It was the worst moment for him in international cricket. Nevertheless, he delivered the goods for Warwickshire on the county circuit, dominating the bowling at a time when Warwickshire swept all before them under former Protea coach, Bob Woolmer. Sadly, bowling for so long at such a pace had taken its toll and in his final Test, against the Australians at the Wanderers in February, 2002, he had to acknowledge that he was injured. However, he came back to finish top of the bowling averages in the Morocco Cup tournament, featuring Pakistan and Sri Lanka. He won Man of the Match, taking 4 wickets for 43 runs against Pakistan, in a contest South Africa won. He was playing well in ODI's too, and showed that he could still remove the opposition's top batsmen, taking 10 wickets in the five-match series against Sri Lanka.

He finally decided to retire after a neck injury prevented him from bowling for his local South African teams – Free State and the Eagles. His career had spanned 19 years and he had represented Warwickshire for thirteen, his tally in limited overs cricket (684 wickets) second only to Wasim Akram, who netted 881. His duel with Michael Atherton, which he views as a career highlight, took place at Trent Bridge in 1988. The two faced each other, neither giving any quarter. Allan, glaring furiously, pulled out every trick in the book to dislodge Atherton and this went on for about 40 minutes. At one point, Atherton was bowled a ball aimed straight at his throat. Putting up his hand and his bat to protect himself, the ball cannoned off his bat, onto his glove and straight to Boucher, the wicketkeeper who caught it. The umpire remained unmoved by the appeal. Atherton stayed at the crease although he knew that, technically, he was out. This turned the match in England's favour and the South Africans lost the series. Some of the fire went out of Allan after that momentous battle, but he and Atherton had a beer together afterwards, Atherton admitting that he knew he had gloved it. Allan agreed that he would not have walked either.

Although now retired, Allan coaches the Warwickshire second XI and assists the Eagles with their bowlers. He is proud to have been part of South Africa's sporting revolution and although he spent a great deal of his time on the international scene, travelling and playing virtually non-stop, he insists, "At least, I've never been bored!"

Allan Anthony Donald
b. 20th October, 1966, Bloemfontein, Orange Free State, South Africa
Right Hand Bat
Right Arm Fast

Sir Richard John Hadlee KBE, MBE

Along with Imran Khan, Kapil Dev and Ian Botham, Richard Hadlee was rated as one of the finest all-rounders of his generation. The 'Master of Rhythm and Swing' as he was dubbed by none other than Sir Donald Bradman, was born on 3rd. July, 1951 in Christchurch, New Zealand where he still lives. His was a cricketing family – his father Walter Hadlee had been captain of New Zealand – and Richard reckons he became a bowler simply because he and his brother Dayle bowled constantly to the other three brothers, who batted. All this took place in the Hadlee back yard, where he used to bowl golf balls as his hand was too small to hold a cricket ball satisfactorily. The golf balls regularly bounced off the wall, which was perfect for catching practice. He pays special tribute to his mother who was wonderful at preparing cricket whites and packed lunches. She was always very supportive, always there to watch and encourage.

Sport was compulsory in schools in those days, he remembers, whereas now it is optional and the children are allowed to take the soft option if they do not feel like playing games. When he was at school, he played rugby, soccer, cricket and athletics, but adds, modestly, that he was nothing special. Cricket became a clear direction for him and he captained the school XI in his last year. When the time came to leave, there was no career path to cricket as a profession and he found himself trainee departmental manager at Woolworths. They could not afford to give him the time off to play cricket but he played anyway, five years as an amateur and also worked five days a week. He first played for Canterbury in 1971-72, forming a solid opening partnership with his brother Dayle. In 1973, he came to England as the youngest member of the Touring New Zealand side, but when the two sides met again in February, 1978, he was at the forefront of the attack at the Basin Reserve, Wellington which saw an England defeat for the first time in 47 years. He took 10 wickets that day including 6 for 26 in the second innings, leaving England all out for 64.

Some of the best years of Richard Hadlee's life were spent at Nottingham, where he lived while he was playing for the county. Clive Rice had joined Kerry Packer and Richard took his place. He married, and was embraced by the club and it was an altogether remarkable time, he says. The cricketing experience with Nottinghamshire, fine-tuned him as a player. When you are playing six days a week, he claims, you certainly hone your skills and learn what you are capable of. He thinks it important that counties should sign up only the very best overseas players, which would help the standard of play. If they are second best, then English players are being denied a chance which could be counter-productive in the long run. His stint with the county and his belief in excellence saw Notts become championship winners and one of the best teams in the country.

One of the secrets to Richard's success was the fact that he was extremely disciplined, methodical in approach and carefully planned how he was going to bowl in any given situation. He was prepared to change his bowling technique, shortening his run. He learnt the hard way, without the network of technical support, physiotherapists, advisers and others that there are today. He feels that, perhaps, players do not put in the hard yards today as they did in the past, preferring to rely on all the support they are given. His way, he maintains, was character-forming and educational. Put simply, he learned a lot.

When the 80s came along, the media built up the rivalry between Khan, Botham, Dev and Hadlee into 'The Battle of the All-Rounders'. "You naturally kept an eye on your opponents to see what they were doing and you lifted your performance," he said. It was a wonderful time, both for them and for the spectators. Richard says that, of all the matches, the one against Australia at the Gabba in Brisbane will always stand out in his mind. He took 9 for 52 and 6 for 71 (15 wickets in one Test), to record New Zealand's first Test win over Australia in 1985/6. There were less wonderful moments in his career, too. In 1978, he was thoroughly embarrassed while bowling to Graham Gooch at Lord's. He tripped over his feet and fell flat on his face. John Arlott, the commentator at the time, described him as being "tall, lean, bit of a stutter in his run, a bit like Groucho Marx stalking a barmaid!" Richard just about managed to see the funny side while Gooch leant on his bat and chuckled. At Bangalore, in 1987/8, he broke the world record for Test wickets, as it stood then, and in 1990, against India, at Lancaster Park, Christchurch, he reached his 400th Test wicket.

Before he had finished playing, unusually, he was given a knighthood for services to cricket, during his final Tour for New Zealand in England, in 1990. He is the only cricketer to have received such an honour while still in the game, and he accepted this final accolade to his career with great pride. He says he knew it was to take place six weeks beforehand, and was done in New Zealand by the Governor-General, but his MBE – awarded in 1981, for services to New Zealand sport – was given to him at Buckingham Palace. These honours were the culmination of the brilliant career Richard Hadlee had carved out for himself by sheer hard work and mental discipline, allied to natural ability. He raised the status of New Zealand to make them a Test side to be reckoned with, principally by his phenomenal bowling. He was a legend when it came to his superb control of pace and swing. However, he could be dangerous with the bat too, curiously, playing left handed, while he bowled with his right arm.

He retired at 39, but he remains active, still determined to be the best at whatever he does. Like most cricketers, he plays golf and does charity work. He has been Bank of New Zealand Ambassador since 1990. He undertakes after-dinner speaking and in his role as Ambassador for the Bank, visits schools and cricket coaching sessions in addition to representing them at fundraising events, client functions and other occasions. His two sons, Nicholas and Matthew, do not take after their father in wanting to make cricket their life. They enjoy playing but not to a high standard. One of the boys, Nicholas, is Secretary/Treasurer for a local club team, but Richard has no expectations that they will excel at the game. When he has finished building his new house, in an alpine resort with hot mineral springs and fishing, he hopes that they will all be able to get away together and simply enjoy being a family.

There is a Hadlee Stand at the old Lancaster Park, his home ground, now the Jade Stadium, named after the family. An annual one-day series is held for the Hadlee-Chappell Trophy, one year in New Zealand and one in Australia. Richard feels he was right to retire when he did. Gone are the physical strains and the pressure of top class cricket and he is pleased with the new direction he has taken. He does a bit of coaching, writes articles and was, for twelve years, involved with television and radio as a commentator. He is now Chairman of Selectors for New Zealand.

Sir Richard Hadlee's contribution to the game of cricket has been immense. In terms of sheer entertainment, in terms of raising the game in his country by his mastery of pace bowling, by his relentless quest of perfection, he will long be remembered as one of the all-time greats, truly worthy to take his place among the legends of cricket.

Sir Richard John Hadlee
b. 3rd. July, 1951 Christchurch, New Zealand
Left hand bat
Right arm fast

Robin Arnold Smith

Robin, 'The Judge' Smith was known as the man who emptied the beer tents. When he came to the crease to bat, nobody wanted to miss it. This large, powerful man endeared himself to the crowds with his awesome batting, mastery of the square-cut and fearlessness when faced with the world's fastest bowlers. Add to this the fact that he was immensely popular for his generosity of spirit and his genuine love of the game and you have a powerful mix.

He was born in Durban, South Africa on 13th September 1963, and from a very early age encouraged by his father, whom he acknowledges as the greatest influence in his cricketing career. He found it a little hard to be dragged out of bed, from the age of 11 onwards, at 5.00 in the morning, to practise in the nets in the back garden, the final exercise being to face 200 balls from the bowling machine before going to school. Discipline and hard work were the watchwords and, at 14 or so, Robin came to appreciate it because he now found that he was better than the others. His father loved sport and was keen for his son to achieve the sort of success he, himself, never had. Hard work began to come naturally. His brother, Chris, who was older by five years played for the Glamorgan second team in 1979 and Hampshire offered him a contract 1n 1980. Robin followed in 1981, encouraged by Barry Richards who persuaded Robin's parents that going to Hampshire was the right decision. As a totally naïve 17 year old, he joined Hampshire on a three week trial, but after two weeks they offered him a four year contract. In order to play for England one day, he had, as someone who had been born overseas, to qualify for four years first. His grandmother was Scottish, which meant that he could play for England once he had qualified.

Robin's nickname 'Judge' was coined in Durban when he was playing club cricket against the University side. Having made 65, one of the fielders who fancied himself as a bowler, shouted "Give me the ball and I'll knock that bloody judge's wig off his head!" The 'judge's wig' referred to Robin's shoulder-length curly hair. The name was cemented when he hit a couple of boundaries off short balls and, relaxing in the bar afterwards, someone called out "Do you want a drink, Judge?"

After signing the contract with Hampshire, he arrived all bright-eyed and bushy-tailed for his first away trip to Glamorgan and Swansea. Mark Nicholas, the captain, was the driver on that occasion and as they approached the Severn Bridge, which would take them into Wales, he suddenly said to Robin, "Hand me your passport, we're coming up to passport control". Poor Robin naturally had not thought to bring his passport and Mark with a straight face told him that it was too late to go back for it and he would have to be smuggled across the border in the boot! Forty-five minutes later, when they had arrived in Swansea, the boot was opened to howls of laughter.

In his first championship match for Hampshire when he was 19, Judge hit a century, going on to help them win three cup finals at Lord's and two National League titles. His record at Hampshire of 23 years devoted service, some of them as captain, has been outstanding, both for the quality of his batting and for his commitment to the team. When it came to playing for England, he averaged 43 in his 62 Tests, with nine centuries. In the first Test against the West Indies at Edgbaston in 1995, although England lost, Judge was the top scorer. As a casualty of the disappointing 1995/96 season Robin lost his place in the Test side and was never to play for England again. He reckons, though, that it had more to do with not being able to play Shane Warne – but then, who could? Most people think that the Selectors got it wrong and he was written off too soon. Nevertheless, he captained Hampshire after being dropped from the England side, which was a consolation, but the way he had been treated had hurt him and he found it hard to cope with. He had to be strong through the transition from Hampshire's old ground to the new Rose Bowl, but being captain meant, for him, not being able to concentrate on his own game. He says that he became much more sympathetic to everyone as a result of the treatment meted out to him, but, perhaps on occasions, he was too nice and was taken advantage of on the strength of it. He admits that over the years, he was a better follower than a leader. He thinks it extremely important that young players must be helped to have a good understanding of what it means to be in a team. Players must behave themselves off the field as well as on, and the Judge readily admits that his own standards, sometimes, fell short of what was required. He tells an amusing anecdote of when he, Gordon Greenidge and Malcolm Marshall were clubbing in Leicestershire, after a match, when a bunch of Welsh rugby players became aggressive towards them. Gordon left and Malcolm and he walked back to the hotel followed by the rugby players, one of whom, made racist remarks and then took

a swing at Robin. He wasn't having any of that. The hugely powerful right arm of Robin Smith smacked him in the face (probably breaking his nose), and then he and Malcolm ran to one of the rooms, just getting inside before the Welsh mob rounded the corner. They cowered behind the door, listening to heavy feet pounding up and down the corridor, trying to locate them. Fortunately, they were unsuccessful.

Nowadays, Robin is totally absorbed in his many and varied business interests. Major Ronald Ferguson, who was passionate about cricket and became a close friend, converted a barn at his home at Dummer into a cricket school and Robin uses it for manufacturing cricket bats. He is into property and many other businesses, as well as after-dinner speaking and hosting all Hampshire's corporate hospitality. Imagine being able to watch cricket, drink and get paid for doing it! During the winter, he takes tours abroad, and has done so for the last nine winters. These trips are for a few, select, cricket buffs and go under the name of 'Judge Tours', naturally. It is so typical of the man that not being able to play for England, he should choose to take people on tour to support the England players, wherever they are. Wherever Judge Tours go, the Barmy Army have usually arrived before them. They are worth their weight in gold for the unstinting support they give to the England players, whom they follow, literally, to the ends of the earth.

The Judge now wants to concentrate on being as good a father as he possibly can to his fourteen year old son Harrison and his ten year old daughter, Margaux, as well as doing his bit for The Lord's Taverners, the Bunbury X1 and for charities in general. He and his wife, Kathy and the children live in the New Forest, which he says is a great opportunity to get away from the real world. When the Judge was in his world, the world of cricket , there was no finer batsman. Viv Richards said it: 'mentally strong on the big occasion, Judgie could sometimes play it like no other.' And you can't get a bigger compliment than that.

Robin Arnold Smith
b. 13th September, 1963 Durban, Natal, South Africa
Right hand bat
Leg break

Sunil Manohar Gavskar

Sunil Gavaskar is a big man in the fullest sense of the word. This may seem surprising since he is small of stature, but his contribution to the game of cricket has been enormous.

Born in Bombay (now Mumbai) on 10th July 1949 the young Sunil was taken to matches by his maternal uncle, Madhav Mantri, who himself had played Test cricket for India. This awoke a passion for the game, which never left him. He began playing in earnest at the age of ten, never giving a thought to any other career and, after graduating, went straight into professional cricket when selected to play for India against the West Indies in 1971.

Many superlatives have been written about 'The Little Master', considered one of the greatest opening batsmen in the history of the game. His technique was near perfect, his agility and quick footwork, coupled with an impeccable sense of timing, saving the day on countless occasions, earning him huge respect. His batting records are truly amazing. In his Test debut in his first series against the West Indies, he notched up 774 runs helping India to win for the first time in the Caribbean. Sunny (as he is known) greatly enjoyed playing the West Indies because of the atmosphere. It was relaxed and colourful. It was also noisy in a good-humoured way and the love of cricket was in evidence everywhere with people flocking to support their team. Such was the impression he created there that a calypso was written about him

"It was Gavaskar the real Master, just like a wall
We couldn't out Gavaskar at all, at all.
You know the West Indies couldn't out Gavaskar at all!"

In 1976 for a brief spell, Sunny became captain of India and again for a longer period from 1978-1985. His phenomenal powers of concentration as well as his undeniable talent and intelligence made him a formidable opening batsman. Nor was he tardy in the field, being arguably one of the best slip fielders of his time.

He admits that his worst moment came when India lost to Pakistan in 1978 in a Test Match he thought was saved, but Pakistan batted superbly and ran brilliantly between the wickets. It had not looked possible that they could win, but they did. In those days the atmosphere between the two countries was always cordial. However, feelings became more intense after 1989. The tolerance level between the two countries lessened to such a degree that the situation was often volatile purely because of politics. An illustration of this came when Tendulkar was given out and it was perceived that the Pakistani bowler had obstructed his return to the crease. All hell was let loose with the angry crowd erupting into violence.

After 1989, India did not play a Test match in Pakistan for 15 years, but in March 2004 a most exciting series took place. India won, and there was no animosity of any kind.

Not only is Sunil renowned for his batting prowess, he is also famous for his headgear. The story behind this somewhat strange fact unfolded in New Zealand when he was acting captain and had posted himself at forward short leg. Lance Cairns swept the ball and, as Sunny started to retreat, he was soundly smacked on the cheekbone. The authorities insisted on taking him to hospital on a stretcher with one of the reserves to accompany him. He was told that he must not close his eyes, so the reserve kept pinching him every so often to keep him awake. Finally, he was informed that he had a broken cheekbone and a depressed fracture of the skull and that plastic surgery would be necessary. In typical Sunny style, he asked the surgeon if he would kindly make him look like Paul Newman! After that incident, Sunny decided to make his own, somewhat eccentric headgear. Luckily he was not hit on the head again, because on examining his home-made protection, an expert on such matters told him that, far from protecting his head, the device would have ensured instant death.

Nowadays he has traded his bat for the commentary box, where he commentates for Sky and Test Match Special when India play. He has also written several cricket books and an autobiography entitled *Sunny Days*.

His son, Rohan, captained Bengal in 2001 and also plays for India, which is a source of great pride. When his son was younger, Sunny relates how Rohan's great hero was the Australian fast bowler Jeff Thomson. "Everything was Jeff Thomson this, and Jeff Thomson that" he said. This irritated Sunny more than a little, especially when Rohan pretended to be a commentator, calling out "Thomson comes in to bowl, a superb ball and Gavaskar is... OUT!"

In the minds of his many fans and admirers, this charming, amusing and urbane man will never be out. He has achieved iconic status, and will be long remembered for his brilliance with the bat and for earning the respect of the world for Indian cricket.

Sunil Manohar Gavaskar
b 10th July 1949, Bombay, India
Opening bat
Leg spin bowler
Slip fielder

Michael William Gatting OBE

cricket's dizzy heights by being a wicket-keeper in his school team. His father had been a club cricketer, and his brother was cast in the same mould, playing for the Middlesex second XI. Mike's enthusiasm for cricket was shared with an equal passion for football. He played for Edgware Town as a teenager, starting as a goal-keeper but also playing centre-half on occasions. He was recommended to West Ham, QPR and offered an apprenticeship with Watford. His brother Steve had a good career with Arsenal and Brighton, but Mike came down on the side of cricket, touring the West Indies with the Young England Cricketers, where much to his amazement, he was required to open the bowling. Prior to that, he had played cricket for Middlesex under-15s and made a century for England schools against Public schools. This then was a sportsman with tremendous natural ability and in 1977, in his first season playing for Middlesex, he made over 1,000 runs, earning his county cap. Mike's Test debut followed in the winter of 1977/78 in Pakistan but it took him quite a while (not until 1984/5) to achieve a score of three figures for England. Once he had got going though, there was no stopping him. Three innings later he had scored, with Graeme Fowler, 207, the highest ever second-wicket partnership score for England.

A little known fact about the immensely popular Mike Gatting is that he won a bronze medal for ballroom dancing at the Neasden Ritz in 1988. It just goes to show that size and shape are no barrier to being light on your feet. It also shows that he had rhythm, an essential component of the batsman's armoury. Born on 6th June, 1957 in Kingsbury, Middlesex, he began his climb to

'Gatt' as he was known, took over the captaincy of Middlesex from Mike Brearley. Brearley had been thoughtful whereas 'Gatt' was somewhat brusque, without much finesse and the first team talk he gave was concise and very blunt. He had always had a healthy appetite and a fondness for pickle, so it was not surprising that he came in for a great deal of ribbing on the strength of it. Middlesex became well-known for the filling nature of its lunches – steak and kidney pie followed by spotted dick and custard – which 'Gatt' appreciated but which tended to overwhelm visiting teams, used to more frugal repasts. On one famous occasion, a visiting Surrey and New Zealand player was violently sick at mid-on and was, in consequence, none too keen to join the others come the tea-break. Diet was, clearly, not high on the agenda. It didn't seem to worry 'Gatt', though, or affect the way he played. All that aside, Middlesex were a good team, used to winning and the new captain was respected and liked, both as a player and as a man. When 'Gatt' came to the crease he presented a formidable sight. There was a swirling of arms and bat, an aggression which dared the bowler to do his worst. The championship in the first year of his captaincy came down to a contest between Middlesex and Essex which they, unfortunately, lost, but which they went on to win in '85, '90 and '93. In 1986 they won the Benson & Hedges Final at Lord's, defeating Kent by 2 runs, having previously won it in 1983. He, personally, topped the batting averages in his first year as captain with 1,373 runs and was named as one of *Wisden's* Five Cricketers of the Year. The following season he made more than 3,000 runs and hit the highest score of his career, 258 against Somerset at Bath. The NatWest Trophy was also theirs, twice, as well as the Sunday League in 1992.

In 1986/7, Mike Gatting became the third England captain to regain the Ashes in Australia. This feat must rank as the highlight of any captain's career, but not content with that he won the Perth Challenge and the World Series Cup into the bargain. In 1987, he led England to the World Cup final, but he was dismissed at a crucial point in the match when he tried to play the reverse sweep. Things went downhill from then on, with his famous finger-jabbing altercation involving Umpire Shakoor Rana, which proved to be one of the most controversial incidents there has ever been in cricket. The following year, 'Gatt' had to step down as captain after another incident, this time involving a barmaid, which was untrue according to him, and accepted by the England committee as such. In 1989, Mike Gatting and fifteen others took the decision to go to South Africa – the Rebel Tour – despite the political situation, with the result that they were banned from international cricket for five years.

It was only when he saw his name come up on Ceefax that he knew, in 1993 that he was back from the wilderness and would be playing for England in India. He had taken some time off after the South African caper, to get his thoughts together, to have a rest and above all, to be with his young family. He was away so much that, when he did, finally, come home his son Andrew would tell everyone that "Mike Gatting is staying in our house tonight." Although he had been prevented from playing for England internationally, he, nevertheless, played for England at Indoor Cricket. He went to Australia to write about the 1990/91 Tour and also to commentate, the following year covering the World Cup. His loyalty to Middlesex mirrored their loyalty to him and he played his heart out for the county, continuing to captain them to a 1990 and 1993 Championship title victory. He tried to set himself personal targets to keep himself up to the mark, aiming a little higher each time, but after several years of not playing for his country, it was not going to be easy. He was far more relaxed about playing for Middlesex and as captain was able to instil confidence into his side. He had a reputation for recognising talent and giving it a chance to flourish, as with Mark Ramprakash, to whom, at 17, he gave the chance to play county cricket ahead of those with prior claims. Mike Gatting bowed out of the Test scene in the 1994/95 series against Australia. His record of 14 county trophy wins as a player is unequalled and he finally retired from first-class cricket in 1998, becoming Middlesex Director of Coaching, a Test Selector and President of the Professional Cricketers' Association.

Mike is also President of the Lord's Taverners for 2005, an MCC Committee member and a committed Trustee of the Cricket Foundation. He has a job as a Sky Sports Commentator and has business interests besides. In fact, he is a busy man. Does he still have a craving for Branston pickle? Quite likely. This splendid 'Best of British', player, with bulldog-like tenacity, has been a huge asset to the game over many years and even now cannot give up his involvement with cricket in the widest sense. The establishment, once fickle in their support of him, have welcomed him into their ranks. Well, times change and people change, along with their attitudes. One thing we hope will never change and that is 'Gatt's' wholehearted commitment to the causes he has taken up. He is about to embark on a 1,000 mile walk in June 2005, starting at the Hampshire Rosebowl, during the England v Australia twenty/20 international and finishing at Lord's on 21 July on the morning of the first Ashes Test Match. What will he get out of it? Sore feet and the satisfaction of having done something for those less fortunate than himself. And to think it all started with ballroom dancing.

Michael William Gatting
b. 6th June, 1957, Kingsbury, Middlesex, England
Right hand bat
Right arm medium

Mark Anthony Taylor AO

When Mark 'Tubby' Taylor decided in February, 1999 to resign from international cricket, the ensuing flood of genuinely-felt tributes demonstrated finally the esteem in which he was held and the void he would leave in Australian cricket.

What sort of man is Mark Taylor? He is a clean-cut, somewhat solid individual who is straight-talking without a hint of false modesty or embarrassment. He exudes dependability and is clearly a man to be trusted. He is very devoted to his wife, Judi, and their three children, William, Jack and Katelyn, and one has the feeling he would rather be spending time with them than doing anything else. He was born in Leeton, NSW on 27 October, 1964 and started playing cricket as a young boy in his home town of Wagga Wagga, about six hours' drive west of Sydney. He continued playing cricket as well as rugby and Aussie Rules football throughout his time at High School and later, University in Sydney, where he passed his final exams and was awarded a degree in surveying. He had been selected to play for NSW in his second year but never thought of playing cricket professionally until picked to play for Australia in 1988. In his first Test against England at Headingley, he made a century and repeated the exercise in his first Test Matches against Sri Lanka, South Africa and Pakistan.

Clearly, here was a force to be reckoned with. Not only was he a masterful opening batsman, but he was also a brilliant fielder at slip who, by the time he resigned as captain, had taken no less than 350 first-class catches.

When Mark took over the captaincy of the Australian side from Allan Border in 1994, he was aware that they had an image problem and he immediately set about building a better relationship with the press and the media. Allan Border had suffered to some extent from the eighties when Australia could do nothing right. Under Mark's excellent and dedicated leadership the atmosphere of the team was transformed. They had started getting into winning ways under Mark's predecessor, but were not behaving quite as well as they could, both on and off the field. Now, with Mark at the helm, leading by example, displaying dignity, sportsmanship and a fierce determination to win, pride in their international side was restored. Australia were the new West Indies and had taken over where they left off.

Mark's brand of attacking cricket was to prove extremely effective against the opposition and exciting to watch. Under his captaincy, Australia won three Ashes series against England, a series against South Africa, the first victory against the West Indies in 23 years and the first series win over Pakistan for 39 years.

Mark has had his detractors, too. In 1998, when playing Pakistan at Peshawar, he made 334 to match Don Bradman's highest score for Australia. Instead of trying to pass this score and beat it, he declared. He said he did this for the good of the team and the result was a draw. He felt he had done the right thing at the time and it shows the measure of the man that he did not seek glory for himself when he could, so easily, have broken Bradman's record. His contemporaries saw him as an outstanding captain, mentally tough and a man who epitomised everything that is good about the game of cricket. One former Australian captain even went so far as to say that he had never heard anyone say a bad thing about him. As with everything in life, timing is all important and Mark Taylor seems to have come along with just the right gifts at just the right time for Australia.

It came as an unwelcome surprise when he decided to retire at the age of 34, but he felt he was losing his edge and his heart was simply not in the game as it had been before. He has no regrets. Now, he happily commentates for Channel 9 in Australia and does advertising and promotional work for certain companies during the winter. Mark no longer plays any form of cricket, preferring to go fishing or play in charity golf matches. Having won the Ashes not once, but three times, and having presided over a glorious revival in Australian cricketing fortunes, Mark Taylor, outstanding player and Test captain, richly deserves his Centenary Medal and his place in the Hall of Fame. The last word rests with Mark and is so characteristic of this supremely modest man. "Cricket has given me more than I have given it". Others think differently.

Mark Anthony Taylor
b. 2 7th October, 1964, Leeton, NSW, Australia
Left hand bat
Right arm medium
Slip fielder

Frederick Sewards Trueman OBE

'Fiery' Fred is 74. Hard to believe isn't it? It seems as though he has always been around, although he officially retired from first-class cricket in 1968, after a memorable career as England's finest ever fast bowler. Born in the village of Stainton, Yorkshire on 6th February, 1931 he was lucky not to have been born 300 yards further down, or he would have played for Nottinghamshire instead of his beloved Yorkshire, as these two counties, were separated only by a ploughed field.

According to his Memoirs his early life seems to have been happy enough, despite sharing the small cottage in a terraced row with his seven brothers and sisters. They were lucky to be in a position to have fresh, home grown food, (his mother baked nine loaves every day), seasonal fruit which was turned into jam and a variety of mushrooms and nuts for the picking. In a poor mining community such as theirs, money was tight and there was never any question of not finishing what was on your plate. If you left anything, it was presented again at the following meal and so on, until it was eaten up. His father was an old-fashioned, God-fearing disciplinarian, we are told, who acquired a certain expertise with horses from his grandfather, who had received a contract from the government to supply the Army with horses to be sent to the Western front. Fred says that his grandfather was a decent cricketer who was invited to play for Yorkshire, but who could earn twice as much in one day trading horses, and declined the offer.

Fred's father rode in point to points and steeplechases for Earl Fitzwilliam, whose stables were at Wentworth Woodhouse. His weight became a problem and he worked at the coalface instead. But horses were more fun and he gave this up to work for Captain Adcock, a well-known racehorse owner at nearby Stainton Woodhouse and was allowed to shoot over his land, so there was always 'posh' food such as pheasant and partridge in season to grace the Trueman table. During the war, his father was awarded a contract to raise pigs for the government, so pork, home-cured ham and black pudding were on the menu quite often. As a child, Fred worked hard as soon as he was old enough, picking potatoes or peas, doing a paper round, in fact anything which would help the family pay the bills. He was a good boy, honest and straightforward, who accepted the way things were, who loved, with a passion, the countryside where he was born and who contented himself with the simple things of life.

One begins to see the influences which moulded Fred and made him the character he became. A character which did not always sit well with people, especially, the cricket establishment. Over a spread of thirteen years, Fred played 67 Tests for England, between 1952 and 1965, becoming the first player in the history of the game to take 300 Test wickets. He was overlooked for England, despite frequently topping the county bowling averages. Fred says that the Selectors thought him 'bolshy' choosing someone whose 'gentlemanly' attributes were more important than their ability to play international cricket. It is probably fair to say that Fred has never suffered fools gladly, or at any rate, those people he thought of as fools.

The first time Fred ever set foot inside a county cricket ground was at Bramall Lane, Sheffield United's cricket club as well as the football club of the same name. First impressions were disappointing because it was not set in the heart of the country, nor was there a single tree only the sight and sound of heavy industry. Net practice was an eye-opener under the excellent coaching of Cyril Turner. It turned out that Fred was not holding the ball properly and, on getting the grip right, his game improved markedly. He was taught how to make the ball swing both ways and he was so pleased with himself that he gave up any thought of becoming a bricklayer – his career choice, hitherto. Having told his boss to "bugger off" (what would Dad have said?) after a disagreement, and getting the sack from the brickworks, the very next day he began making tiles on a machine, which was so unstimulating that he moved on to a glassworks, where a decent wage was to be earned making bottles.

Cricket became more and more important to him. Although his performance had been patchy, he had taken enough wickets to impress and he was invited to Leeds to be coached during the winter by Bill Bowes and Arthur Mitchell, the latter a wonderful coach who had the greatest influence on him. He was stunned by the size of the pitch at Headingley and even more stunned when the legendary George Hirst stopped to talk to him. He sat, uncomfortably, waiting to hear his fate after bowling eleven balls, three of which had hit the stumps. It was not until he was on the bus going home that his father informed him he had been picked to play for the Federation team, which would be touring the south of England. One of the lads on the team was Ray Illingworth, who felt travelsick the whole way, and the others took turns in trying to comfort him, a glimpse at the camaraderie to come, even though they were so young.

By 1948, Fred was playing for the Sheffield first team in the Yorkshire League and knew that he wanted to be a professional cricketer. He was earning the unbelievable amount of £6 a week, which when supplemented by a collection – if a bowler took 6 wickets for under 25 runs – meant that he sometimes came home with the princely sum of £12. A fortune. During the course of an after-dinner speech, the great Herbert Sutcliffe remarked that cricket in Yorkshire was in good hands as they had players like the young Fred Trueman whom he predicted would play for Yorkshire before he was 19 and for England before he reached 21.

Yorkshire had asked Fred to get a job in a 'reserved occupation' in order to avoid National Service, so he took a job at the colliery at Maltby. He was soon picked to play for the Yorkshire First XI and the initial game, against Cambridge University proved to be an education in more ways than one. He said he felt a 'stranger in a strange land' when it came to dinner at the University Arms. French menus, gentlemen players with savoir-faire and dining etiquette all conspired to make poor Fred feel very uncomfortable. It was after this match that *Wisden* produced its howler of the century, writing that Fred Trueman was a slow, left-arm spin bowler! Playing Oxford next, he took 6 wickets for 72 runs and heard the umpire say that he would end up playing for England. To be a genuine fast bowler, says Fred, every part of your body must move smoothly and rhythmically and he adds that he has no doubt that it was his ability to swing the ball that contributed to his success.

Being chosen to play for Yorkshire at Lord's, the hallowed home of cricket, set Fred's pulses racing. Walking out to bowl, he was filled with pride and by the end of the day had taken eight wickets for seventy runs. *Wisden* now referred to him as a fast-medium bowler after that match, but Fred, himself, never faltered in his belief that he could make the grade as a top fast bowler. There followed a spell out in the cold, with no contact by the Yorkshire authorities, and it was this indifference on the part of the powers-that-be which made him forever wary of the cricket hierarchy. It was at this time that the nickname 'Fiery Fred' was coined by Norman Yardley. Fred loved to indulge in a bit of sledging, telling the batsmen that they wouldn't be there long. He felt it his duty to try and remove the batsmen in any way he could. Unfortunately for him, others didn't. In 1951, Fred was hailed as the fastest bowler in English cricket. He would send a ball whistling past an opening batsman's ear to get him onto the back foot where he had more chance of being caught. As luck would have it, some batsmen were hit and while Fred felt sympathy for them, he wasn't going to show it. There were never any hard feelings afterwards, quite unlike the two-faced approach of some at Yorkshire. After other clubs had made overtures to Fred, he finally got his county cap. He went home, put it on to show his father and never wore it again. It belonged to his Dad. He promised his mother his first England cap and kept his promise.

By 1952, the press and the public were calling for Fred to be included in the England team, but National Service had caught up with him and he was in the RAF. Nevertheless, he was picked to play for England against India at Headingley. Len Hutton was to be the first professional captain of England in the history of the game and there was a fantastic crowd for this Test, which proved to be a very well-matched encounter. England won and 'Fiery' Fred came of age. The rest of his well-documented career saw a total haul of 2,304 wickets in Test, County and other First-Class matches, probably more than any other fast bowler in the history of cricket. He always claims that the proudest moment of his career was not in a Test, but when he led Yorkshire to victory over the touring Australians at Sheffield in 1968, after which he retired. Although his cricket career had gone from strength to strength, his private life was increasingly difficult. After a marriage which had produced three children and boded so well at the beginning, the strains of being a cricketer's wife, with a husband who was hardly there, took its toll and he and his wife, Enid parted for good. It was an extremely unhappy time for Fred, but he kept it to himself and redoubled his efforts to support children's charities. This is a little-known side to him, but he has raised a great deal of money, over the years for children in need, something which had started almost at the beginning of his career. Perhaps having such a happy home life as a youngster, made him feel keenly that not all children are so fortunate.

In the early seventies, Fred became a member of the respected Test Match Special team, along with John Arlott, Brian Johnston, Don Mosey and Trevor Bailey. At various times, E. W. Swanton would provide excellent close-of-play summaries. Christopher Martin-Jenkins and Henry Blofield joined the team later on. For more than twenty years, Fred had written a weekly column for the *Sunday People*, cricket in the main, but also some football. His marriage to Veronica, his best friend, has lasted more than thirty years and the relationship keeps getting better and better, he says. He is in demand as a speaker on the after-dinner circuit, with a fund of amusing tales from his cricketing days, which never seem to go stale. There is no doubt that Fred Trueman is a singular man, out of step with this modern age of cricketers who hug each other every time a wicket falls. A nod to the batsman and a nod back was quite enough in his day. As an unemotional Yorkshireman (in public, at any rate), although highly sentimental at times, brought up the hard way, he must think how spoilt and pampered they all are, particularly when they travel, and how different it was then. He values loyalty above almost any other attribute except for plain-speaking. He is a plain-speaking man himself and has little or no time for those who do not say what they mean and mean what they say. He has often found himself in hot water for being a little too blunt for some tastes, especially when he has a microphone in his hand! Having been brought up to be frugal has coloured his views and he is nothing, if not careful, with his money now. Not having had the chance to play for England as much as he would have liked has left a bitter taste, but at least he can be secure in the knowledge that England has rarely produced such a fine fast bowler, nor Yorkshire a worthier son.

Frederick Sewards Trueman
b. 6th February, 1931, Stainton, Yorkshire, England
Right hand bat
Right arm fast

COUNTY GENTLEMEN

John Robert Troutbeck Barclay DL

Johnny Barclay, or 'Trout' to his intimates on account of his middle name, was born in Bonn, Germany on 22nd January, 1954, where his father was a diplomat. On returning home, the family lived at Horsham, Sussex and it was here that Johnny discovered his fascination with the moving ball, which he remembers always trying to hit. At five he saw his first cricket match at the famous ground at Horsham. He recalls that he was intrigued by the sets of stumps at each end and that he liked the look of the smart caps the cricketers wore. He wanted to position himself where he could pick up the ball, should it come his way. Children are very much influenced by sport and Johnny was no exception. His grandfather Troutbeck and his uncle, Lancelot Troutbeck, who taught at Westminster school, both played cricket. Although his father was not keen on the game, his mother became interested and equally, his elder brother. He was particularly influenced at his pre-prep school in Brighton by 'Sir' (he never knew his name). 'Sir' loved cricket and was a marvellous teacher, taking 12 boys to the playing fields to practise. There were occasional matches and one in particular, sticks in Johnny's mind. They batted first and were all out for the grand total of 4. Johnny managed to score 1 run, which he felt was a triumph.

He was captain of the first X1 at his prep school, Summerfields, with some success. At Eton, too, he was captain of the first X1, but felt that there was too much emphasis placed on elite sport and not enough on music and art, though this has now changed. When he left school, Johnny, by now completely obsessed by cricket and longing to play for Sussex, structured his life round the game. He had played for the county while still at school, then at 18 he played for them professionally as a good all-rounder. He spent six months in Hong Kong as a stockbroker, but after a huge surge in the market, followed by a slump, Johnny found himself out of a job. However, he was detached enough to become interested in what made people gamble – from risking vast amounts on the Stock Exchange to having a small flutter at the racetrack.

Johnny's mentor and greatest influence was the captain of Sussex, Tony Greig. Although not everyone's cup of tea, he was an outstanding leader and a tremendous champion of the young. He captained England, but was not a particularly good tactician however, he made up for this by being very good with people. Once, when facing fast bowler Andy Roberts while playing Hampshire, Greig had said to him, "I am really pleased you are opening the batting. You are just the man to sort out Andy Roberts!" Johnny, grew even taller that day. In the fullness of time, he became captain of Sussex and was proud to have Imran Khan in his team. Imran tried hard, practised hard and took terrific pride in his game. He was a tremendous asset to the side and the reason Sussex almost won the championship. Dermot Reeve, too, started out with Sussex and was subsequently a great captain of Warwickshire. Johnny continued to play for Sussex until 1986, when he felt he had had enough. He had captained Sussex for six years and he knew he was, now, never going to play for England.

Just as one door shuts, another invariably opens and an opportunity presented itself in 1985, while Johnny was playing at Canterbury in August. The telephone in the dressing room rang at five minutes to eleven, just before the start of play. "Colin Cowdrey for you, Trout" said someone. It was indeed the great man and he outlined an idea he had for Arundel involving youth cricket. "Would you be interested in running it?", he asked. "Yes", replied Johnny, then forgot about the conversation. Just after Christmas that year, Colin rang again and asked him to come to tea with Roger Gibbs whom he already knew. The whole family went to discuss the project, as it would mean moving and an upheaval. It was decision time. He felt he was ready to move on to a less commercial atmosphere than the business he was currently in, and the time had come to settle down into a job which would be more of a vocation. The concept of teaching and helping youngsters to develop was far more to Johnny's liking. He started putting the project into motion in November 1986. He had long been dismayed that school sports no longer took place and that playing fields were being sold off by councils to raise money and that successive governments simply were not interested in sport in schools. Add to this, a succession of powerless sports ministers and it is not difficult to see how too many children are deprived of sport in a way which is totally detrimental. The Arundel Castle Cricket Foundation was born.

Sir Paul Getty made them a magnificent donation to start the project off and they acquired some dedicated Trustees to steer the ship. The children have come, largely, as a result of contacts in London, principally the London Community Cricket Association run by John Smith. The Foundation, locally, runs a schools' programme of coaching, the children staying near Pulborough in an excellent Youth Hostel. They are aged between 8 and 16 and are, on the

those from independent schools, who pay for their coaching sessions.

Johnny took a sabbatical for three or four years while managing different England teams, particularly the 1996/7 tour of Zimbabwe. He managed the under-19s when they went to Sri Lanka in 1993 with Michael Vaughan as captain. He says he became adept at failure in those days. In 1994 he went to India, 1995 South Africa and 1996/7 Zimbabwe and New Zealand. Johnny observed how mentally fragile his players were when the unexpected happened, although Zimbabwe are tough players and this was a timely lesson.

MCC matches take place at Arundel under the auspices of the ECB and a good, close relationship with everyone must be maintained. However, all these matches must be fitted in round Arundel's own busy cricket programme.

The most pleasing aspect for Johnny is the feedback he gets from those who have spent a week at Arundel. They have loved the cricket and the surroundings (and who could fail to be impressed by such a beautiful ground), and the gentle encouragement they receive. This has a good influence on many, though not all. The pressures on these children from drugs and other things can be overwhelming at a very vulnerable time in their lives, explains Johnny and if we can help them in a tiny way, then that is what it is all about.

Johnny Barclay, with his shock of dark hair rather like Harry Potter, is a remarkable man whose own privileged upbringing and education have led him

whole, good boys and girls. Johnny also works with special needs schools and it is of great benefit to these children, who love it. There are, naturally, occasional lapses of good behaviour and some problems, but it is part of the project to overcome these. Notable successes of the scheme are Alex Tudor and Tony Paladino who bowls for Essex.

Funding is a perennial problem. Money comes from grant-making Trusts mainly and from government organisations when possible. The Foundation has also had modest success with the National Lottery. The indoor school, built with the Getty donation, has been used by more than 150,000 children since completion, including

to devote his time and energy to helping others, less fortunate than himself, in the way he knows best; by teaching and encouraging them through sport to adopt a healthier approach to life, both mentally and physically and to stop and wonder for a moment at the beauty of God's creation of which they are all a valued part.

John Robert Troutbeck Barclay
b. 22nd January, 1954 Bonn, Germany
Right hand bat
Right arm off break

Alexander Colin David Ingleby-Mackenzie

Colin Ingleby-MacKenzie first broke cover on 15th September, 1933 at Dartmouth Naval College, a somewhat surprising venue, even for him. His father was a naval captain at the college and a keen cricketer, who played for the Navy. Doubtless, he encouraged in his young son a liking for the game, but it was Mr. Honeyman (who sounds like a character out of an E. M. Forster novel) bowling at Colin for hours on end, who was his real inspiration.

At Ludgrove, his prep school in Berkshire, the headmaster Mr. Barber (father of Gerald, the present head), by great good fortune was passionate about cricket and enthused Colin and did all he could to help him play to the best of his ability. Competitive matches were arranged with other prep schools, notably Sunningdale, and Colin's time at Ludgrove seemed to pass very agreeably indeed. On to Eton, where it was clear that he possessed a good deal of talent, although he never captained the first eleven. His father by this time had become an Admiral in charge of Haslar R.N. at Portsmouth and Colin was coached in the holidays at nearby Southampton by Jim Bailey. During one of these sessions, his coach suddenly without warning called over Desmond Eagar, captain of Hampshire. Colin was bowled a few friendly deliveries which he disposed of well and was immediately asked whether he would consider playing county cricket. The idea grew in him and he found himself, eventually, in the Hampshire team. The first time Colin ever captained a side was in 1957. He and Desmond Eagar shared the captaincy until he took over at the age of 24 in 1958. He was considered a personality to be reckoned with in county cricket and voted the best young cricketer of the year.

Colin states, ruefully, that he should have won the championship that year, finally carried off by Surrey, but the whole team seemed to be suffering from an attack of the jitters. If only they had relaxed, he feels, they would have won. These close calls did Colin a lot of good and gave him the mental approach for 1961, when Hampshire did win, under his inspiring leadership. His players would do anything for him, such was his charismatic personality. There was much speculation in the press that Colin might be taking a side to Australia, but Ted Dexter, captain of Sussex, was chosen in his stead. Although, doubtless disappointed, Colin being the character he is, would have taken all this in his stride and not have allowed his personal feelings to affect the team. They were extremely fortunate to have two world-class players at that time, Derek Shackleton, the bowler who played for England and Roy Marshall, an overseas player from the West Indies. He captained three overseas tours, twice to the West Indies and a world tour, organised by E. W. Swanton, ending in Calcutta. It was a great thrill for him to have Garfield Sobers and Richie Benaud in his side for this tour.

It is, certainly, correct to say that Colin, coming from the era of gentlemen and players, was an amateur all his cricketing life and he found it a distinct advantage to be independent of the club, as he then had more control over what he did. His only rule, as captain, appeared to be: 'Be in bed by breakfast time'. Outside cricket, Colin did a great deal. He tended, then at least, to burn the candle at both ends and it is a wonder he found the time to sleep. On one occasion, when Hampshire had beaten Oxford, he and his great friend and kindred spirit Leo Harrison, the wicket-keeper, hurriedly changed into morning coats and sped off to Royal Ascot, where they had been invited to join Stanhope Joel, millionaire racehorse owner and breeder in his box and afterwards at dinner at The Compleat Angler in Marlow. After being well fed and watered, they left at about 4.30am to drive back to Southampton where they were staying with Desmond Eagar, arriving at 7am, just in time to get into their beds with their clothes on before being unceremoniously hauled out again by Desmond who asked them if they had slept well. Unknown to them he had heard them return and when they answered in the affirmative, he told them he knew they had only just come back. He made them get up and ferried them to Bournemouth for a match. Colin slept all day until someone shook him saying urgently, "Skipper, you're in". He picked up his bat and proceeded to make a century in 61 minutes, the fastest 100 of the year! Colin won a prize of £100 and the J. Walter Lawrence Trophy with which he was highly delighted. When asked, in later years, what his philosophy for a good life was, Colin is reputed to have said, "wine, women and song". Certainly, this attractive, witty and charming product of a bygone era seemed to live life to the full and what is more to the point, thoroughly enjoyed doing it. He whiled away many a happy evening at the Clermont Club with John Aspinall and Lord Lucan, living life in the fast lane. Living life in the fast lane almost always involves racehorses and, true to form, Colin has a share in several decent animals, both national hunt and flat, trained by Lady Herries, Sir Michael Stoute and

Mick Channon. He has known certain moments of great luck, admitting to being a bit of a gambler and loving the excitement and adrenalin rush which having a winner can bring. It was said of Colin that, sometimes, he cared more about the racing results than a change in the bowling!

Colin plays a good deal of golf and was captain of Sunningdale in 2000. He is Chairman of Saints and Sinners (the Prince of Wales being a notable member), a charity founded by Percy Hoskins, crime correspondent for the *Daily Express*. The one requirement for membership is that prospective members must be 'raffish'. An old-fashioned word if ever there was one. 'Disreputable, but in an attractive manner' is the definition in one Oxford dictionary. The main purpose of Saints and Sinners is to raise money for small charities struggling for donations. They give away about £100,000 annually to several small organisations, raising this large sum by holding a prestigious golf tournament, the main donor being Cecil Redfern. This philanthropic gentleman makes up the difference between the proceeds of the fundraising events and the figure needed to meet whatever target is set. Sir Donald Gosling also organises a fundraiser every year, last year's being held at Highgrove.

With all his activities, does Colin have a home life? In 1975 he married 'Storms', alias Susan, who brought four children to the marriage and they have one daughter together. Susan's nickname does not derive from hysterical outbursts (although, she is very likely entitled to them), but from her previous name of Stormonth Darling. Perhaps she is known as Darling Storms as she seems to be the perfect foil for him. His friends, too, mean a great deal to him and

it was Colin who gave the address at his friend, the late Robert Sangster's funeral last April, saying "It is now sadly the end of a chapter of delightful scams, and tasteful skulduggery and generosity..." They had the same love of life and shared many interests in common. Robert Sangster bred the fantastic Sadler's Wells, the best-known sire in racing today, as well as owning and breeding many other top-class horses

Colin's sense of fun was matched by his sense of fair play and this has made him a highly popular figure in the cricket world. Although Colin retired from first-class cricket in 1965, forty years on he could not be more involved. He was an expansive and popular President of the MCC for two years (usually a one-year appointment), and was largely responsible for the admission of women members to Lord's, and is now President of Hampshire Cricket. In his cricketing days, Colin was acknowledged as a superb all-rounder practising hard to turn himself into an excellent fielder. He was a swashbuckling left-hand batsman, a right arm off-break bowler and a wicket-keeper. As with cricket, so with life after cricket. His life is, evidently, still full and well-rounded and, judging by his youthful appearance, capacity for laughter and his quick-witted remarks, time has not yet, quite caught up with him.

Alexander Colin David Ingleby-MacKenzie
b.15th September, 1933, Dartmouth, Devon, England
Left-hand bat
Right arm off-break
Wicket-keeper

FIRST LADY OF CRICKET

Rachael Heyhoe Flint MBE DL

"I never asked for it – it all just happened". These words of the remarkable Rachael Heyhoe Flint seem at odds with her rise and rise in the cricket world, a male bastion if ever there was one, to become the first woman elected on to the Committee of the hallowed MCC. Surely, she must have pushed, just a little bit, somewhere along the line?

Rachael was born on 11th June, 1939 in Wolverhampton, Staffordshire, to parents who were both PE teachers. Curiously, her mother and father had met in Denmark, at a PE college in Copenhagen, where her father was a lecturer and her mother a student. To qualify as a physical education teacher in the 1920s and in Denmark, must have made Rachael's mother a very unusual woman indeed. Both Rachael's parents were good at tennis and hockey and her father had played for an amateur soccer team in Denmark. It was hardly surprising, then, that Rachael was destined to become a sportswoman. All she knew from the earliest years was sport – playing with her brothers and their friends in the garden. In the winter, her father played hockey to a high standard and Rachael attended these matches, insisting on 'having a go' herself, afterwards. Summers were reserved for cricket and her father, who was a reasonable club cricketer, set the example. By this time, her brother and friends had to put up with her joining in their matches and batting far better than any of them. After one game, when she batted undefeated for three days and 380 runs, they declared that the cricket season was over and the football season had begun! She progressed to Wolverhampton Girls' High School where she played a variety of team games. As luck would have it, her school played cricket which was unusual for girls in those days. One of the teachers played cricket herself and founded the Wolverhampton Ladies' Cricket Club which Rachael joined at 14.

Cricket has been played by women since at least 1785 when the first recorded match took place. Ladies' cricket matches drew large crowds and were the subject of wagers between gentlemen. Over-arm bowling is said to have been invented by Christine Willes, to avoid her billowing skirt which would have impeded an underarm delivery. Her brother claimed the credit and spent much of his life trying to get overarm bowling accepted. It was to be nearly two hundred years on, in 1934 that there was a first England Women's Test match, resulting in the defeat of Australia at Brisbane.

Rachael was accepted at the Dartford College of Physical Education after leaving school, choosing speech and drama as her supplementary course. As luck would have it, Mary Duggan, one of the staff at the college, was also captain of the England Women's Cricket Team. Ruth Westbrook also on the staff was the national wicketkeeper. Rachael became cricket captain of the college and was selected for her first overseas tour, to Holland with a WCA (Women's Cricket Association) squad. In her final year, 1960, she was chosen to go on a WCA cricket tour of South Africa (by Union Castle line, irreverently known as Cattle Line). By 1966, she was captain of the England Women's team. Funding had been a problem in the women's game for some time as had the lack of publicity and enthusiasm by the public at large. Meanwhile, Rachael had moved to journalism after teaching PE, where her English A-Level stood her in good stead. She was determined always to select the best team, not simply those who could afford to go abroad as had been the case hitherto. While on tour, herself, she had sent pieces to Reuters about the touring England Women's side, making telephone calls on her return, constantly trying to keep women's cricket in the public eye. She became PR Executive for women's cricket with a brief to encourage sponsors and get them coverage. St. Ivel came on board in the late 1960s and in 1976 there was a St. Ivel Cream Jug to be played for. She must have been doing something right because in 1970, she received a letter inviting the team to play in the West Indies, addressed simply to Rachael, Edgbaston CC, England. Enter Sir Jack Hayward (known as 'Union Jack'), the great British philanthropist who had bought Lundy Island, but who lived in the Bahamas. He rang Rachael and agreed to sponsor the women's team, asking "How much do you need?" He gave them the airfares and a bit of spending money as well and this was the beginning of a great friendship with the Hayward family. Jack was also responsible for financing the first indoor school at Lord's.

Jack further suggested a World Cup of Women's Cricket and sponsored it. In 1973, the first ever Women's World Cup was held, the final consisting of England v Australia, played at Edgbaston, and Rachael and the team were the victors. It was an extremely proud moment for her when she received the cup on behalf of the Women's Team, from Princess Anne. Without Jack Hayward and the West Indies tour, none of this would have come about. As a result of this high-profile match, the women's game received more sponsorship and in Rachael's word, they "got going". In 1977, after eleven years at the helm, and after winning the World Cup without dropping a game, Rachael herself was unceremoniously dropped from the team. She was, in all likelihood, a victim of her own success. She had become a household name and the fact that she appeared on the front page of her local newspaper seemed to signal to the Association that she was getting all the credit, was far too high-profile at the expense of the rest. Sir Jack resigned as Patron in protest and there was such a furore that an extraordinary general meeting was called. A vote was passed of 'lack of confidence' in the committee. Rachael was never given an adequate explanation for her dismissal as captain and it must rank as an act of treachery by those she had served well, for the greater glory of the women's game, not the greater glory of Rachael Heyhoe. She cannot help being bubbly and extrovert and it was precisely these attributes, coupled with her ability to play top-class cricket, that endeared her to the average (and not so average) person and made her name synonymous with women's cricket. She was reinstated in the team in 1978, not as captain though, and continued playing until 1983, when full-time journalism beckoned.

Rachael has one son, now 31 and three step-children. They are an extremely supportive family in everything she does, particularly the Lady Taverners, the fund-raising arm of the Lord's Taverners, which has 900 members, all with good contacts. The Prime Minister of the day is always an honorary Lord's Taverner, but when it came to Margaret Thatcher, several cricketers' wives got together to form the Lady Taverners and she became the first Lady Taverner. They have raised huge sums of money for various activities to do with young people and children with special requirements.

Rachael was in the news again over the issue of women members of MCC. When Colin Ingleby-MacKenzie became President of MCC, he was determined to sweep away prejudice against women. This preserve of male privilege (as it was seen by some), had their minds wonderfully concentrated by the fact that the Sports Council turned down the request for a big grant for a new grandstand at Lord's, because MCC was seen as a private, exclusively male club, not giving equal rights to women. In the end,

they decided to name ten women honorary life members, of which Rachael is one. After being on the Marketing Committee, she was elevated to the main committee – the first woman on the committee in 217 years. This wonderful lady has never had to apply for a job. She fell into a PR job with the Godfrey Davis Group after Cecil Redfern had seen her at a roadshow. Having honed her PR skills on women's cricket, she felt she could cope with anything. She now does PR exclusively for Wolverhampton Wolves, a women's soccer team. The La Manga club in Spain has involved her as a consultant. She is Deputy Lieutenant of the West Midlands, deputising for Royal occasions and the swearing-in of magistrates. She is a witty and entertaining after-dinner speaker, always in great demand. If her autobiography is anything to go by, she has more than a few amusing tales to tell. Apparently, the late Harry Secombe told Rachael to call her autobiography *Tit Willow*!

'Flinters', as the very wonderful, late Brian Johnston used to call her, has been a sparkling asset to the game of cricket. A small, delightfully extrovert woman, now in her sixty-sixth year, she shows no signs of stopping. Good for her. Her presence on the committee of the prestigious MCC can only do women and the game of cricket good. She isn't all fund-raising and PR, though. Guess what she has an interest in now? Feng-Shui.

Rachael Heyhoe Flint
b. 11th June, 1939, Wolverhampton, Staffordshire, England
Right hand bat
Commentator

THE UMPIRES

Harold Dennis Bird MBE

Dickie Bird

Ask anyone, even those who know nothing about cricket, to name an umpire and the answer is always the same – Dickie Bird. What has made this Yorkshireman such a household name? One can guess, but not be certain. One thing is certain, though, he is one of the great characters of English cricket and his occasionally quirky behaviour is seen as, well, just Dickie.

Dickie was born on 19th April, 1933 and as a youngster, his parents insisted that he go to Sunday school and later, church. His Christian faith, he says, has helped him throughout his career. He called upon the Almighty regularly before Test matches when he was due to umpire, "Dear Lord, please no rain and above all, no bad light!"

Dickie's antics with the light meter were well-known, and as far as wet weather went, rain seemed to follow him round wherever he tried to do his job. Not just rain, either. On more than one occasion, he had to cope with sodden ground. It became a nightmare to him. At Headingley, when England were playing the West Indies, the groundsman had blocked up the drainage system, quite deliberately to keep moisture in the ground. Unfortunately, he had not reckoned with torrential rain, which then waterlogged the pitch. The staff at Headingley worked hard through the night, to make play possible the next day. Fortunately, the sun came out early, drying things up, and with a good sprinkling of sawdust, play started only half an hour later than scheduled. Ambrose bowled to Gooch, first, second, third time and suddenly Dickie heard a voice, "Mr. Dickie, come back here man, we have got big problems." Halfway through his run-up, water welled up from the ground until it covered Ambrose's boots. The captain, Viv Richards, said they would have to go off. "Go off?" expostulated Dickie, "they'll slaughter me." But go off they did and Dickie heard the crowd saying "You're here again, Bird, you're bringing them off, again." Poor Dickie, he began to get a complex about watery skies and waterlogged pitches.

Again, at Old Trafford, England v West Indies, he brought them off the field, past the members' enclosure and could hear snatches of "You're here again, Bird, bringing them off; blue skies, sunshine, what is your problem this time?" "No problem, Sir, it's lunchtime!"

Dickie, like so many young boys was encouraged to play cricket at school and inspired and enthused by one of the masters. When he left, at 15, he went to Barnsley cricket club in the Yorkshire League. His cricket was of a high enough standard to see him signed up to play for Yorkshire at 19. He scored 181 not out against Glamorgan on one occasion, when none of the others made many runs at all, and typically, he was dropped for the next match. He moved to Leicestershire as he was unable to get a regular place at Yorkshire. "We were a good side in those days", he adds with pride. By the time he had

finished playing first-class cricket, he had notched up 3,000 runs.

He began his umpiring career at the age of 37 and made the first-class umpires' list in 1969. In 1972, he was appointed to the Test Match panel and never looked back. Dickie's punctuality is legendary, principally because he arrives a good three to four hours before the off. The fact that the gates to the ground are firmly locked and he has to climb over them, doesn't come into the equation. His philosophy is simple: get along with everyone and earn the respect of the players. Over the course of his career, he seems to have done just that, so much so that wherever he goes in the world, he always has someone to take him out and entertain him. Or should it be Dickie who does the entertaining? He has a wealth of amusing tales, all perfectly true, if a little embellished, and he is great fun and good value when on song. There is, however, another side to our Dickie. He cares terribly about the state of his health – "I have high blood pressure, you know, it runs in the family", and very often, if not always, travels, business class of course, with his own supply of food. Yorkshiremen of a certain vintage clearly have trouble with spicy food and it's best to be on the safe side.

He manages to squeeze liquorice allsorts, mars bars and gingerbread men into his suitcase on the off chance that he might need something sweet and recognisable. Food notwithstanding, Dickie loves going to all the cricketing nations – India, Pakistan, the West Indies, Australia and his favourite place of all outside England, New Zealand. In India, should he walk in the streets of Mumbai, Calcutta or Lahore, he is instantly recognised and people greet him and ask him into shops, wherever he goes. They love cricket there and, of course, all the boys play it, unlike boys in England these days.

Dickie had a spell working in the fitting shop of a colliery while playing for Barnsley CC, so he is very familiar with coal mines and the deprivation that surrounded them. There is a lovely, heartwarming story of his great friend, Sir Paul Getty and the Miners' Strike. The coal miners' wives came to Dickie after the strike was over to give him a plate they had had specially made, to hand to Sir Paul. Why? Because Sir Paul Getty had, unknown to anyone, put bread on their tables during those bleak days when their menfolk had been out of work and desperate. When Dickie gave him the plate at Wormsley, Sir Paul had tears in his eyes. He has umpired many times at Wormsley and was with the Getty family at the Memorial Service held for Sir Paul when he died. Friendship means more than anything to Dickie. He does admit to having been in love, twice, but on thinking it over, realised that he was wedded to cricket. He lives in a seventeenth century cottage, sleeping in the room where once John Wesley slept and is wonderfully looked after by his devoted sister.

Dickie is the only man in history to have umpired the Women's World Cup as well as the Men's, on the occasion when Rachael Heyhoe Flint played in New Zealand and Australia beat England in the final at Christchurch. He does not altogether approve of 'newfangled' electronic aids. He feels that they undermine the authority of the umpire. He was brought up to make his own decisions and if you have a good umpire, you don't need a match referee. He can't abide mannerisms either. A short tap on the leg is quite sufficient for a leg bye, and there is no need for an all-over massage. All you need to be a good umpire, in his opinion is dedication, application and common sense and above all, concentration. It is not an easy job, standing about for six hours, watching like a hawk. "It's all about money today", he sighs, "money, money, money." The characters seem to have disappeared, too. Everyone is so earnest and intent on making money, money, money.

Apart from writing an impressive number of books (his autobiography has sold a million copies), he has set up The Dickie Bird Foundation to help underprivileged children of all persuasions. The Patrons are Sir Tim Rice, Michael Parkinson (with whom he used to open for Barnsley) Sir Bobby Robson and John Major. Dickie is a great fan of Johnny Barclay who runs The Arundel Castle Cricket Foundation, an organisation trying to do much the same sort of thing, through the medium of cricket.

His awards and accolades are legion – Freedom of the Borough of Barnsley, Honorary doctorates at Sheffield and Leeds, and an MBE in 1986 (he thinks at the instigation of Mrs Thatcher). On that occasion he was invited to 10 Downing Street to receive his award. He has had a fulfilling career, but made no money out of umpiring, though his literary efforts have earned him a bob or two. The players, especially the likes of Lamb and Beefy, have been the delight and the bane of his life, but through it all, this often faintly eccentric character has upheld the spirit of the game, entertained the crowds, and brightened even the dreariest of summers with his own brand of irrepressible Englishness. The crowds loved him, the players respected him and with his white leather cap (specially made for him in Australia), his affinity for water and his treasure trove of funny stories, he will go down in cricket lore. At his final Test appearance at Lord's in 1996, against India, the players formed a guard of honour and the crowd gave him a standing ovation. Dickie was moved to tears.

Harold Dennis Bird, MBE
b. 19th April, 1933 Barnsley, Yorkshire England
Right hand bat
Right arm off break
Umpire

David Robert Shepherd MBE

In Bideford in the beautiful county of Devon, on 27th December, 1940 an umpire was born. Of course nobody knew that at the time. He didn't look like an umpire straight away, but looks can be deceptive. He came from a sporting family, his brother Bill a good cricketer, was on the groundstaff of MCC for three years after leaving school. There was plenty of sport going on where they lived at Instow, a village in North Devon. It had a good cricket ground and a beach, which became a playground in the summer. The headmaster encouraged David to play sport and he was fortunate to have such good, committed teachers.

In his second year at Grammar School he made the first XI, though he was the smallest by miles. He was forced to make up for his lack of size, and therefore, lack of power, by developing his skills. He was so small that he was known as 'Titch'. At the age of nine he was asked the usual daft question, "What do you want to be when you grow up? Would you like to be a professional footballer?" "No, Sir". Undaunted, the teacher tried again, "A professional cricketer?" "Oh, yes Sir", not knowing what it would be like. Thus Shep set his heart on being a cricketer. The teachers at his school must have been an enlightened lot to ask a young boy whether he would like to play games for a living!

In the fullness of time, Shep received invitations from Kent, Lancashire and Somerset for trials. His father insisted that he have some sort of qualifications to fall back on, just in case things did not work out. Shep duly qualified as a teacher at St. Luke's College, Exeter and taught sport as well as other subjects for four years. He thought he had missed the boat so far as cricket was concerned, but lady luck was smiling and he was spotted while playing for Devon, by a scout from Gloucestershire. He had a trial in 1964 and was offered a contract beginning in 1965, which, not unnaturally, he jumped at. He played fifteen seasons for Gloucester, by all accounts being one of the most popular players ever to represent that county. All those Devon cream teas and excellent home cooking had taken their toll, even then, but this did not stop him from making a century on his debut or from being an effective and powerful middle-order, right hand batsman. He was capped in 1969 and earned a Benefit in 1978.

What to do when he had finished playing? Ex-cricketers sometimes become umpires in order to stay in contact with the game, on the other hand he could always do a spot of coaching. He was offered a coaching job at Gloucestershire, but decided to have a go at umpiring instead. In 1981, he began first-class umpiring and was marked by the captains. Luckily, he had only just finished playing, himself, and he knew a fair proportion of the players, which helped. It was good to have gone through the playing experience as it meant they all talked the same language. He admits to being very nervous before his first big match, Oxford v Leicester. The first day was rained off, but Shep learned a great deal from talking to the other, more experienced umpire. He advanced up the ladder to umpiring in the 1983 World Cup and, in 1985, umpired his first Test match at Old Trafford, with Dickie Bird. It was England v Australia and the captains were Allan Border and David Gower. England went on to reclaim the Ashes and Shep was particularly impressed with Border's attitude, which he said was magnificent.

Dickie got Shep to go abroad, to Sharjah, which he enjoyed, but not the heat. He now has to go all over the world. As the only Englishman on the ICC panel, he is precluded from umpiring at home to avoid any bias. As if there would be any, with an umpire as fair-minded as Shep. In world cricket there is a panel of eight full-time umpires, selected by the ICC. There are four umpires at Test matches, two standing, a third umpire/TV umpire and a dogsbody/referee. They are looked after very well when they go abroad. Shep particularly likes Australia and they like him, too – a lot. New Zealand is good and he finds himself with cricket people all the time, which adds significantly to his enjoyment. They are always extremely hospitable to him in India.

Standing on one leg, when the score is at 111, or any triple, has become Shep's trademark. In English cricket, the bogey number is always 111, in Australia it is 87. The only way to avoid anything bad happening is to get a foot off the ground. Someone wrote into Johnners at Test Match Special about this idiosyncrasy, which he promptly broadcast to the world. During a Test match at Lord's, the late, great Brian Johnston was asked if he would mind wishing Shep's mum, a postmistress, a happy birthday. "A Jolly Happy Birthday", he said as only he could. Another game at Lord's, England v Australia, with wall to wall sunshine and everything going swimmingly when up went a roar from the Nursery End – there she was, as nature intended, a streaker charging straight for him and he knew his mother would be watching. She did one cartwheel,

then another, whereupon he put his hands over his eyes, until the stewards could get her off the field. There he was, the umpire, in the hot sunshine, shielding his eyes and a naked girl beside him, upside down. Should he have listened to Colonel Stephenson, Secretary of MCC when he said, "If you see anyone preparing to streak across the field, pounce on them!"

Shep is often asked if he has painted anything lately? The public at large obviously fail to realise that David Shepherd, the distinguished artist of countless magnificent wildlife paintings (mostly in David Gower's collection!) and David Shepherd the umpire, are two different beings. Sometimes he is asked when he gave up being a Bishop. occasionally, he and the late Bishop of Liverpool, the Rt. Revd. David Sheppard, used to receive each other's letters. Once, on a Tour to Zambia, billeted out with ex-pats, they wanted to know where the Reverend was as they had lined up a church service for him to conduct. A certain John Shepherd played for Kent before being signed to play for Gloucestershire. Shep was asked if he was his son. "No", came the tongue-in-cheek reply, "He's the black sheep of the family. Good player, played for the West Indies and a very nice person". It must be part of the job spec. that umpires keep a fund of amusing anecdotes, ready to trot out at a moment's notice. Certainly, Dickie Bird has them rolling in the aisles with his tales of water, water everywhere.

Shep is of the opinion that there is not as much fun in the game as there used to be. He is not alone in thinking that way. The players have to be a great deal fitter and they don't drink and socialise so much. They are all much more intense and earnest and he thinks this is because of the one-day game. The public like it because it moves along quickly and it is usually a sell-out, whereas seats for Test matches are not always filled. The ICC knockout competition, India v Pakistan at Edgbaston, was sold out within half an hour.

When things go wrong for Shep, he is mortified, especially when his mistakes are verified by Hawkeye and the television. Once when this happened to him, he had his nose rubbed in it the next day, as he was delivering newspapers (yes, he has a paper round for his family's post office/newsagent business). The headlines leapt out at him. "England would not have lost, but for his decision." Eddie Nichols, the West Indian umpire had missed a few, too. He felt like throwing in his white coat. He rang Tim Lamb at the ECB about his position, but got nothing but support from him. Friends, players and the public all encouraged him to stay on. Once he was asked if he wanted a drink, swiftly followed by, "Would your dog like one too?" implying he was blind, but he doesn't mind that sort of leg-pulling at all.

David acknowledges how good the game has been to him. He has had a lovely life, first playing, then umpiring, meeting many famous people – The Queen, who gave him his MBE, Mother Teresa, Princess Diana and several Prime Ministers. One thing he cannot abide, though, is a cheat. Having tremendous respect for the game and all that surrounds it, himself, he expects everyone else to feel the same way. He is flattered when the Selectors ask him whether, during the course of the season, he has seen any likely players, or what he thinks of a certain player. He is a totally natural, down to earth character, who has given his all to the game he loves and whose portly figure, instantly recognisable, has endeared him to everyone watching cricket over the past twenty-six years. This marvellous man, now in his mid-sixties, flies all over the world, upholding the best standards of umpiring, always in a courteous and good-humoured way, respected, even loved and then, when he returns, it is business as usual down in Devon and David Shepherd, MBE gets on with delivering the newspapers. It could only happen in England.

David Robert Shepherd
b. 27th December, 1940, Bideford, Devon, England
Right hand bat
Right arm medium
Umpire

PRESENT PLAYERS

Andrew John Strauss

orn in Johannesburg on 2nd March 1977, Andrew Strauss, also known as 'Lord Brocket' (because he's posh and that's as far as the resemblance goes) and 'Barry Big Pants' (why?), has become a very bright star in the English cricket sky in a very short space of time indeed. Last year, in May 2004 at Lord's, he made 112 in his maiden Test innings against New Zealand and you can't have a better start than that.

As a young boy of six, his parents moved to Melbourne and that is where he was first conscious of having played cricket, or rather, whacked a ball. He was mad keen on all sports, but rugby and cricket in particular. His early education began at Caldicott, a prep school known to have a strong games tradition, where Andrew learnt the fundamentals of cricket and where it became increasingly important to him. At this stage he was rather small for his age but as he grew taller and stronger, he found he could hit harder. At his public school, Radley, also an establishment with a strong games tradition, he spent three years in the First XI, and was captain in his last year. Coaching at Radley was excellent and so were the facilities. He is amused to think that Andrew Balding, his head of house, son of a famous racehorse trainer is, himself now a trainer of repute, having taken over from Ian Balding, his father. Andrew Strauss is bright. He took and passed 4 A-Levels achieving 3 A's and a B in History, Economics and Politics, and two Mathematics subjects. At Durham University he read Economics, and when he left he was already contracted to play for Middlesex. It was a case, then, of trying to get into the First XI, but there were quite a few decent batsmen around, notably Mark Ramprakash and, of course, Mike Gatting.

During his first summer at Middlesex, he admits he really struggled and averaged about 30 playing for the second team. This was something of a wake-up call and it made him realise that to play professional cricket you had to act in a professional manner and treat the game with respect. He started going to the gym and getting himself fit, taking care to eat the right things, and being fit physically made him feel mentally that he deserved to do well because he had worked so hard. At the same time, he had to get his batting technique on course. Graeme Fowler, a summariser for Test Match Special and an ex-England and Lancashire player, helped him greatly at Durham. In 2003, Andrew took over the captaincy of Middlesex and having had three or four years at county level he felt ready to go on to the next challenge. He was becoming adept at dealing with the media, and felt comfortable in the big arena and reasonably comfortable off-pitch as well. He found the time he spent at the England Academy at Adelaide very useful. Instead of trying to find that elusive, magic formula which would turn him into the batsman he had always wanted to be, he realised that he had to be himself, not copy anyone and learn to accept his limitations. He soon learned what worked for him.

Being captain of Middlesex, had forced him to think about cricket more – "you start thinking about the team as a whole, planning for the best outcome and until you are in the position of captain, it does not really dawn on you to do this." He has the greatest admiration for Michael Vaughan who is very level-headed and does not get caught up in hype but just gets on with the job and is very enthusiastic. He brings a sense of discipline and a sense of fun to the team and the England side is a very happy ship on the strength of it.

His first time at Lord's, playing for Middlesex, was incredibly special for Andrew. The tradition of the place, the ghosts of past great players and the feeling that he was one in a long line of famous men who had felt the magic of the occasion, was something he will never forget. His Test debut was, undoubtedly, the icing on the cake. He only played because Michael was injured and was fortunate to be in the side on a day when everything gelled, a day which kick-started the rest of his career. And what a career

it has been to date. The Test in South Africa in 2004/5 revealed 'an organised mind in control of a solid defence' and an amazing ability to pile up the runs without being overly flamboyant. In the first test at Port Elizabeth, he made a century and was Man of the Match, helping the England side to their eighth successive Test victory. He formed a solid opening partnership with Marcus Trescothick and to have beaten South Africa (ranked second behind Australia) in their own country, winning the Series 2-1, was a tremendous effort and bodes well for the forthcoming Ashes series, beginning at Lord's in July. Although Andrew's game seems more suited to Test cricket than anything else, he has done brilliantly in the one-dayers too. He scored a century in a one-day international against the West Indies at Lord's in 2004 and gave the statisticians a treat, being only one of a select band to achieve a century on both his ODI and Test debuts playing on the same ground.

Andrew Strauss is learning to live with the 'waltz' label. Every other headline seems to say something like 'Andrew Strauss waltzes to his century' or Andrew Strauss, Waltz King'. He does not think he is related to Johann Strauss, elder or younger, but he takes it all in his stride and hopes that, maybe, they will get fed up with the same old line. One thing is sure, he will go on making headlines for a long time to come. In October, 2003, he married Ruth, an Australian girl, in Australia. He was picked for the one-day internationals, left England on a Wednesday night, arrived in Australia on Friday, got married on Saturday and left for Bangladesh on Wednesday. The honeymoon had to be postponed! They now live in Ealing, London. Andrew says that you need to get away from cricket for a while or it begins to take over and you start worrying too much about low scores. He maintains "it sorts itself out if you don't become too obsessive." This remarkable young man is a wonderful role model for any aspiring cricketer. He has worked very hard to improve his game, his humility and willingness to learn are impressive and his level-headed acceptance of defeat (not much of that, yet) as well as victory is in the best traditions of the game. He has known how to make the most of his opportunities and, as a result, is England's top-ranked batsman and tenth in the world – surely captain material. He is extremely personable, can laugh at himself and exudes dependability. He is a fine individual and the England side is lucky to have such a dedicated and loyal servant.

Andrew John Strauss
b. 2nd March, 1977, Johannesburg, South Africa
Left hand bat
Left arm medium

Michael Paul Vaughan

There have been numerous milestones during Michael Vaughan's career, each one spurring him on to ever greater achievements. In 2001, he scored his first Test century against Pakistan at Old Trafford, then 115 in the first Test at Lord's v Sri Lanka in 2002, another century in the England v India, first Test at Lord's the same year, but in the second Test, at Trent Bridge v India, he received a hero's ovation, playing the innings of his life, a magnificent 197, striking 23 boundaries and inspiring England's huge total of 617. Again, at the Oval in the fourth Test v India, he just missed out on a double century. In Australia 2002/3, he became the first visiting batsman for 32 years to top 600 runs. At Lord's in 2004, against the West Indies, he made a century in each innings. Before that, Michael Vaughan's England side had defeated the West Indies in the Caribbean for the first time in 36 years, starting the run of eight consecutive Test wins which culminated at Port Elizabeth in December, 2004. Twice in one year he had lifted the Wisden Trophy. However, the summer of 2003 delivered the ultimate accolade which Michael, himself, endorses. "There is no greater honour than to captain one's country", he said after his appointment, which came in unexpected

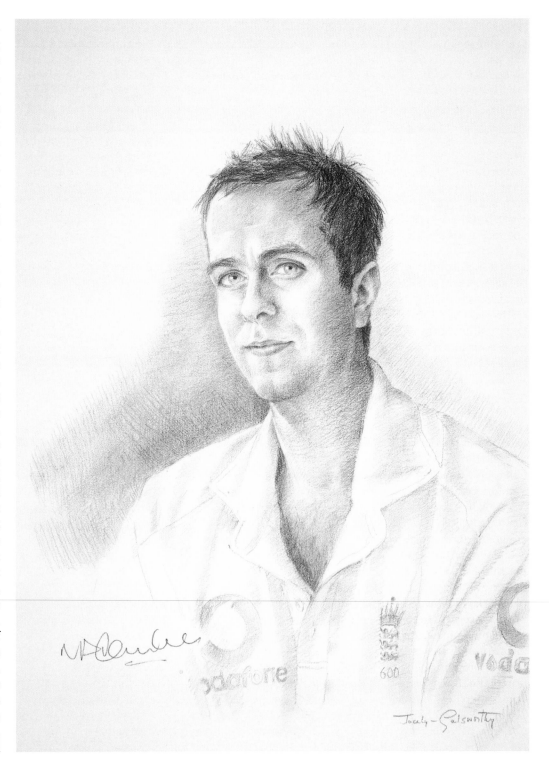

circumstances, following Nasser Hussein's sudden resignation. Not content with one celebration, Michael had a second when he married Irish-born Nicola the same year. A mere two weeks earlier, he had become captain of the England ODI side. Michael's rise has been in a steep upward curve and he is not done yet. He is patiently determined to achieve the very best standards for himself and for the England side, and he has made a fair fist of doing so already.

His selection as England captain came as no surprise. Michael Vaughan was already a batsman of undeniable quality. His skill as an all-round sportsman marked him out at an early age as someone who was likely to succeed. Born in Manchester in 1974, his family moved to Sheffield when he was a young boy. Like so many before him, he could equally well have been a professional footballer if he hadn't taken up cricket. One way or another, he was determined to be involved in sport. He played cricket for Yorkshire in every junior age-group before signing a contract with the county. He was the first cricketer who had not been born in Yorkshire to be given a contract, which brought him and the county a great deal of publicity. Typically, he dealt with this publicity in the level-headed way which has marked him out ever since. He made his debut for the county in 1993 in a Roses match at Old Trafford, scoring 64 against Lancashire. His loyalties lay with Yorkshire, declaring it to be "the best county to play for, not just because of its traditions but because it provides such a good learning curve if you are going to play for England. You come across the odd, disgruntled character, but that stands you in good stead."

Michael has a languid elegance which belies his capabilities. At the crease he is correct and somewhat upright but has moments when he sparkles, particularly when he executes the cover drive which is something of a trademark. Nasser Hussein, his former captain, said that he would pay to watch him bat. He has ceded his place as opening bat to Andrew Strauss, but both of them have dogged determination and patience for the long game. He is famous for being able to put the previous delivery out of his mind and to bring total concentration to the job in hand. Sometimes, though, like that supremely elegant player David Gower, he can fall prey to the daft dismissal.

However, cricket being an individual game, played in a team environment, the key is to focus on the end result. So much of cricket is in the mind and it pays to be mentally strong. His renowned calmness and cool calculation does not make him insensitive to the need for the vibrant atmosphere of the arena, though, and he pays special tribute to the Barmy Army – England's loyal band of supporters who are always present to lift the spirits of the England team.

In the two years that Michael Vaughan has been captain of England, he has managed to create a happy, hard-working, professional side with the will and the skill to win matches. He has given them a belief in themselves by getting everyone involved and communicating with each other. New players are made to feel welcome, which was not always the case before. He is of the opinion that central contracts have done a huge amount to foster cohesion in the team and to encourage players not to think of the individual, but of the team as a whole. Important as cricket is, it is not life and death and Michael does keep a sense of proportion about what is, after all, only a sport. He is aware, however, that he and the team have made a difference to people's lives over the past year or so. The Test and ODI results have been so encouraging that his next big battle, the Ashes, whoever wins, will be fought by two evenly-matched teams for once. For all Michael's charm, good looks and calm demeanour, he is a tough nut when the occasion arises. He is not slow with the verbal volleys on the field, (although sledging has no effect on him) and he will organise his field the way he wants to, regardless of the media and other well-wishers. He and Duncan Fletcher, the England coach, work well together and what the team does, or does not, do will be up to them. What the team has done lately is show character and determination, vital ingredients if they are to stand up to the Aussies.

Not every waking hour is spent thinking of that urn, locked away at Lord's. He is the father of a little girl, Tallulah, whom he probably finds hard work but adores, he plays golf off a 10 handicap and sees the possibility of working in golf management one day. As long as his job involves sport in one form or another, he will be happy. He is heartened by the fact that there are initiatives to bring schoolchildren into cricket and his own attitude to the game sets a fine example. "I would tell a young player that he would have the opportunity of meeting people, of travelling to fantastic places and of learning to be independent. But the first thing I'd ask him would be whether he enjoyed the game."

Michael Paul Vaughan
b. 29th October, 1974, Manchester, England
Right hand bat
Right arm off-break
Captain of England

Ricky Thomas Ponting

As the two captains of the Ashes teams get ready to face each other in July, 2005, Ricky Ponting (also known as 'Punter') may well be wondering if his bet is safe. The Australians know that they will be facing one of the best England sides in recent years and you can be sure that their preparation has been meticulous and intense. After a summer of solid wins in the southern hemisphere, only beaten by India, Ricky is not looking to let his guard down. He has ordered his bowlers to have regular net sessions, instead of putting their feet up, so as to avoid any possibility of injury. He knows full well the importance of his quick bowlers and does not want anything to go wrong. The batsmen, on the other hand, of whom he is one, can afford to take a break.

Ricky, now 30, is a phenomenal right hand bat and an equally awesome fielder. He was acclaimed by Rod Marsh, the Academy coach as the best teenage batsman he had ever seen. He began in Tasmania, where he was born, first playing competitive cricket in school at 8 or 9. As far back as he can remember, he wanted to play cricket for Australia. Legend has it that his grandmother bought him a T-shirt when he was four, with the words 'Inside this shirt is an Australian Test Cricketer' printed on the front. Prophetic or what. At the age of seventeen, he represented Tasmania and on his Test debut at 20, narrowly missed his century, making 96 before being given out. He is aggressive at the crease, playing every shot in the book, but favouring the hook, the pull and the square cut. He hits his attacking shots hard and his defensive shots only marginally less so. His dead-eye fielding is breathtaking at times as he moves with lightning speed, leaving the opposition wondering what happened. He is rated as the best in the world in the crucial backward point area. As a batsman, Ricky also stands alongside the best.

On his first ever Ashes Tour in 1997, he made 100 in the first Test at Headingley, on the way to an innings win for Australia. The year before, he had played three Tests against Sri Lanka in Australia and two against the West Indies, after which he was dropped. His career at that point was somewhat up and down and with a few off-field indiscretions, he admitted to having problems. These are all behind him now and his demons have all been exorcised.

In 2002, Ricky inherited the one-day international captaincy from Steve Waugh, leading Australia to a crushing victory in the 2003 World Cup, where he made a match-winning, undefeated 140. His style of cricket is particularly suited to the one-day game. In 2004, he became the first Tasmanian captain of Australia and there could be no bigger accolade or recognition of his talents than that. He is a popular captain who communicates well and does not entertain defeat. His positive attitude and belief in himself, coupled with his undiminished enthusiasm for the game, is infectious to the rest of the team. He has an imaginative cricket brain, but is at the same time, relaxed, fun-loving and easy to get on with. The team know each other really well, he says and understand each other's personalities. Ricky is well aware that a captain is only as good as his team, which is self-evident,

but the team need a captain they can rely on, look up to and one who is a good manager of men, someone who will get the best out of them. Ricky seems to fill those requirements admirably.

He is married, to Rianna, but they have no children as yet. What he does have, though, is around thirty greyhounds, which he also breeds. They are situated in Melbourne and Tasmania. His father and grandfather owned racing greyhounds years ago and Ricky seems to have caught the bug. He has a share in a racehorse, too. Of course. He doesn't have the nickname 'Punter' for no reason. Luckily, there is a greyhound rehoming society which will find suitable new owners for greyhounds whose careers in racing are over. He loves the MCG as 'it is such an awesome stadium' in his words. It is sensational to play to a full house of 80-90,000 people. Ricky, then, is a showman, delighting in the big occasion and wanting to please the crowds. He will have plenty of opportunity to do that on the Ashes Tour, which he acknowledges is the most special of all Tests.

Ricky's wife, Rianna, travels as much as she can on behalf of the Children's Cancer Institute and they are both Ambassadors for this research organisation. She has become a large part of their fundraising efforts, holding charity dinners in Sydney and Melbourne, raising 600,000 dollars for the work of the Institute.

This dynamic and very likeable Australian has won 27 Man of the Match awards and was *Wisden's* first Leading Cricketer in the World for 2003. Like the captain of 'the old enemy', he has presided over an unprecedented run of successes and the meeting between them will be nothing if not highly charged. The teams are well matched, for once, and it could go either way. One thing is for sure, Ricky Ponting will be leading from the front. But he is at pains to point out that, for him personally, it is not how many runs he scores, important though that is, but how he plays the game.

Has he made any plans for the day he retires? He will only go so far as to say that he won't coach. Golf will, surely be on the agenda – Ricky plays to scratch or one, regularly. He has already written a book – *World Cup Diary* – and is launching another on his captaincy, so perhaps there will be one more when the dust has settled. "Hopefully," he grins, "something will come up". There is no doubt that it will because, as Ricky points out, "when you are captain of Australia, the world is your oyster."

Ricky Thomas Ponting
b. 19th December, 1974, Launceston, Tasmania
Right hand bat
Right arm medium
Captain of Australia

Andrew Flower

Andrew Flower marked his last international series for Zimbabwe in the World Cup by wearing a black armband to protest against 'the death of democracy' in his country, alongside fellow Test cricketer, Henry Olonga. He wanted to bring to the attention of the cricketing world, at least, the plight of his countrymen, both black and white, under Robert Mugabe's increasingly tyrannical regime. "Don't get me wrong", he says by way of explanation, "land reform had to come, but not that way". He is, clearly, passionate about his country but feels that he cannot return for the foreseeable future.

Born in Cape Town on 28th April, 1968, one of five children, four of whom were boys, there was always someone to play with after school since the whole family was keen on cricket. Andy loved sports of all descriptions but felt he was best at cricket. After his education, he worked for a year as an accounts clerk. It would be hard to imagine a more unsuitable job for a young man such as Andy. An offer then came for him to play club cricket in England. He had always wanted to travel and his wanderings took him, eventually, to Holland where he lived for two years.

In 1992 Zimbabwe achieved international Test status and, along with his brother Grant, he made his debut in a one-off Test against India in Harare, which ended in a draw.

Andy had two stints as captain, leading Zimbabwe to their first Test victory against Pakistan in 1994/5 and becoming the first Zimbabwean to lead a Test tour to England in 2000. He was acknowledged as his country's only batsman of genuine Test quality and one of the best players of spin in the world. In 2000 he was named as *Wisden's* Cricketer of the Year and there followed a wonderful period when he was so consistent that he earned a place as the finest player his country had ever produced.

However, there always seemed to be an underlying current of dissatisfaction with the powers that be and Andy found himself leading the protest against the Zimbabwe Cricket Union's disregard for better pay and benefits for the cricketers. Meddling in politics was not Andy's style, but fighting against what he perceived as injustice was part of his makeup and he could hardly help himself. He was suspected of being the ringleader in the cricketers' threats to strike. When Andy Flower and Henry Olonga stood up to be counted in 2003 to draw the attention of the whole cricketing and non-cricketing world to the injustices being suffered by their people, they wrote themselves into the history books for their courage and determination. No one doubts that it has cost them dear in their personal lives, but they have earned the admiration of all for the stand they took together.

Andy does not feel able to predict what the future holds for the Zimbabwean team. "In 1999, we had a good, organised side" he says. "It is anybody's guess as to which way it will go now". The infamous quota system is one which is difficult to stomach.

It is acknowledged that domestic cricket in Zimbabwe is very weak and in consequence the national side has suffered embarrassing defeats. Until politics take a back seat, it is hard to see from where the improvement is to come. Grant, too, left Zimbabwe in 2004, announcing his retirement from international cricket after finding himself acting as a courageous spokesman for the players. He has signed a contract with Essex and the two brothers are together again, as they were in Zimbabwe

In 2003/4, Andy played for the South Australian Redbacks, but he also signed with Essex and was undecided as to where to make his home. He chose to settle in England and bought a house in Essex where he lives with his wife and family. His association with the county has earned him much respect, both on and off the field.

He keeps himself fit by scuba diving, playing squash and parachute-jumping. In fact, Action Man has nothing on Andy. He loves all forms of extreme sport and is "willing to try anything". This does not mean that he is all brawn and no brain. On the contrary, Andy is a somewhat introverted and reflective individual who used to read a great deal and clearly thinks deeply. When the time comes for him to retire, he has already laid the groundwork for a possible coaching career by taking coaching qualifications. That is what one calls forward planning. Perhaps he might join Henry Olonga in a musical career, if only he could sing. Whatever Andy does, he is just the sort of determined man to make a success of it.

Andrew Flower
b. 28th April, 1968 Cape Town, South Africa
Left hand batsman
Right arm off break bowler
Wicketkeeper

Adam Craig Gilchrist

What has happened to wicketkeepers these days? They simply do not know their place. They think they are batsmen, and the funny thing is, they are. Adam Gilchrist, or 'Gilly' to his friends, is a case in point.

Adam was born in Belligen, New South Wales on 14th November, 1971 and always wanted to be a wicketkeeper, ever since falling in love with a pair of green and white gloves he spied in a shop window. However, it was as a middle order batsman that he started his one-day career and only took up the gloves when Ian Healy retired. Healy had been Adam's mentor and the finest keeper he had ever seen. Nevertheless, comparisons being odious, Adam decided to be his own man and not copy or imitate the style of his predecessor. To this day, Healy gives him advice from the other end of the telephone and he also consults Tim Nielson, the Australian assistant coach, who used to keep for South Australia.

Gilly made his mark in England in the first Test at Edgbaston in 2001, when his remarkable 152 not out from 143 balls, culminating in a late order stand with Glen McGrath, completely foiled the England side. He hit 20 fours and 5 sixes in this swashbuckling innings. In the same series, when he was made captain of the Australian side owing to Steve Waugh's injury, he was severely criticised for declaring too soon and allowing England to win at Headingley, thanks to Mark Butcher, giving the Poms their only taste of success in that Ashes series. He thinks that Ricky Ponting has exactly what it takes to be a good captain and will probably go down in the annals as one of the great captains of Australia. Adam is still vice-captain and his versatility as both wicketkeeper and batsman must give the Australians a head start. Stepping in for the injured Ricky Ponting, he led Australia to their first series victory in India for thirty five years. Following his example, teams all over the place are now looking for Adam Gilchrists, but the truth is that he is a phenomenon, perhaps unique, in that his talent is natural, born not made. Despite having God-given talent, he has worked hard as well to get to where he is today.

There is something more about Adam than just being a brilliant batsman and a wonderful wicketkeeper. He has an old-fashioned sense of fair play, charming manners and is modest to boot. He walked, despite being given not out in the 2003 World Cup semi-final against Sri Lanka, and continues to do so, whenever the occasion arises. This is not team policy, merely Adam's personal choice. In New Zealand, when Gilchrist caught McMillan, who had appeared to get an inside edge off Jason Gillespie, the confident appeal was turned down by Umpire Bucknor. McMillan, caught on the stump microphone, was heard to say, "Not everyone has to walk, Gilly." Gilly must have smiled to himself when McMillan was out lbw next ball. However, just because he plays in what he interprets as the true spirit of the game, does not mean that he is soft on his opponents. "I don't ever want to be involved in a team that hands the Ashes back to England," he declares. With the gauntlet thrown down, or in his case, on his hand, the Poms had better look out!

Gilly is a devoted family man and would love to be able to spend more time with his children. He also sponsors an Indian child, Mangesh, through World Vision. He insists that his children be brought up with good manners and respect for their fellow human beings, and they certainly have a role model in their Dad. He has announced that the 2007 World Cup is likely to be his last series for Australia as the feeling of wanting to be with his wife and children keeps on growing in him. We'll see.

Adam Gilchrist is one of the superstars in the cricket sky; a hard-hitting batsman of undeniable quality, a tireless wicketkeeper, making 15 runs more per innings than any other keeper in history. Some say that it was this man's arrival on the Test scene which changed Australia from powerful to overpowering. That may be so, but the quality of the entire Australian team, both as players and as people, has impressed the whole cricketing world. They will be sure to start favourite for the Ashes series, but it's not over 'til rain stops play and the only certainty is that spectators round the Test grounds in England, in the summer of 2005, are in for a rare treat.

Adam Craig Gilchrist
b. 14th November, 1971, Bellingen, NSW Australia
Left hand bat
Right arm off-break
Wicketkeeper
Wisden Cricketer of the Year 2002
Wisden Australia Cricketer of the year 2002/3
Allan Border Medal 2003

Matthew Lawrence Hayden

atthew Hayden was born at Kingaroy, Queensland on 29th October, 1971. His father owned a peanut farm where they lived and his mother taught music and speech therapy. It was here that the young Matthew first picked up a cricket bat at the age of two or three. He got along very well with his brother, Gary, who was five years older than Matthew and the two were so close that they never seemed to fight. They both loved cricket for which they had a natural talent and spent many hours at home both practising and playing. Matthew recalls that he was greatly encouraged by his parents in his enthusiasm for the game and they used to regularly drive him to matches which took them five hours to reach, thinking nothing of undertaking such a trip.

At the age of fifteen, he caught the eye of an A-Grade team in Kingaroy when he was playing at a cricket carnival. He was invited to play for them but he insisted that he would do so only if his brother could play too. They both played and Gary ended up with the higher score. This was not, however, shades of things to come as it was Matthew who possessed the strength of mind and the determination to make a career out of first-class cricket, while Gary chose a different path. As Matthew himself admits it was only through hard work and dedication that he has made it to where he is today.

Today he is a left hand batsman of devastating effectiveness, having made the world record Test score of 380 against Zimbabwe at Perth in October 2003. This record stood for only a short while until Brian Lara eclipsed it by making 400 not out in the England v West Indies series in April 2004. Both men instantly congratulated the other by telephone, Matthew saying to Brian that at least his record was beaten by one of the two the best batsman in the world, the other being Sachin Tendulkar. In 2003, Matthew was named *Wisden* Cricketer of the Year for 2002/3 having already won the Allan Border Medal as Australia's most outstanding Test player of the year 2002. It is not too much to say that he is thought of by many as one of the greatest batsmen in the world – another Don Bradman in fact. After a slow start to his Test career, he was dropped from the team and it is likely that he would not have been recalled were it not for the intervention of Steve Waugh who, recognising Matthew's outstanding ability, insisted on having him in his team. Suddenly, beginning in 2001 and the tour to India, a new Matthew came to the fore. He started making confident Test

hundreds and his average shot up to above 73. Unusually in a batsman, he became much more imposing and intimidating at the crease, his mere physical presence on the field somehow seeming threatening to the other side. As an opening batsman in partnership with Justin Langer, he has shared more double-century opening stands than any pair in history, battering and sledging his opponents into submission. Matthew relishes confrontation, riling the bowler and standing outside his crease or advancing down the wicket to show his contempt for even the fastest bowlers in the world.

After a spell in the doldrums when he could hardly hit anything at all and his future hung in the balance, he was back to his impressive best in the one day internationals against New Zealand in February 2005. His old confidence had returned and the team had its opening bat in top form once more. In putting on 133 with Ricky Ponting, he set his side on the path to victory and displayed his characteristic heavy hitting straight drives and pulls, much to the delight and relief of his many admirers.

Matt creates quite a stir off the field as well as on. He is a tall, blonde, well-built, good-looking Aussie with intense blue eyes and an easygoing, affable manner. It is truly endearing that he talks about his wife Kellie and their beautiful little daughter, Grace almost more than any other subject. At the moment of writing they are awaiting the birth of their second child. In this respect, Matt is very much the 'New Man', not afraid to show the softer side of his nature – a nature he is very careful to keep hidden on the field. Unwisely, perhaps, he allowed an Indian numerologist to examine his palms and among other things, he was told that he had a loving nature and a childlike innocence. He is, certainly, a man who is capable of displaying humility and is extremely modest about his achievements, and as such is an excellent role-model for young, aspiring players. Nevertheless, he has always believed in himself, right from the early days at Valleys District Cricket Club, Brisbane, through to first-class cricket for his state, Queensland in 1990-91 and then on to Test cricket as part of the Australian team. So devoted was he to the baggy green that rumour has it he even took it to bed with him! As he himself says, "I have been blessed with a rich journey, full of ups and downs from which I have learnt". He is mentally very solid and can now laugh at what he terms his worst moment in his cricketing career (tame compared to others) during the 1995/6 Test against the West Indies. Facing a ball from Curtley Ambrose, he decided to leave it. He realised instantly that he had made a big mistake. The next thing he knew, the off-stump went flying down to the wicket-keeper leaving poor Matthew feeling very foolish and not a little frustrated. The fact that all eyes were on him as he walked back to the dressing room merely rubbed salt into the wound.

In his cricket life, Matthew has collected the nickname 'Jurassic', for what reason no one knows, or if they do they are not telling... He has recently published a cook-book, full of recipes from his travels with the Australian team, which may seem a little surprising, but which fits in well with Matthew's take on life in general. He is certainly not what one thinks of as the stereotypical male from Down Under, for all that he enjoys surfing almost as much as playing cricket. And fishing is high on the agenda, too. Wherever there is water, that is where Matt is at his happiest. Which Matt will we see on the Ashes Tour? A bit of both would be ideal.

Matthew Lawrence Hayden
b. 29th October, 1971, Kingaroy, Queensland
Left hand bat
Right arm medium bowler

Darren Scott Lehmann

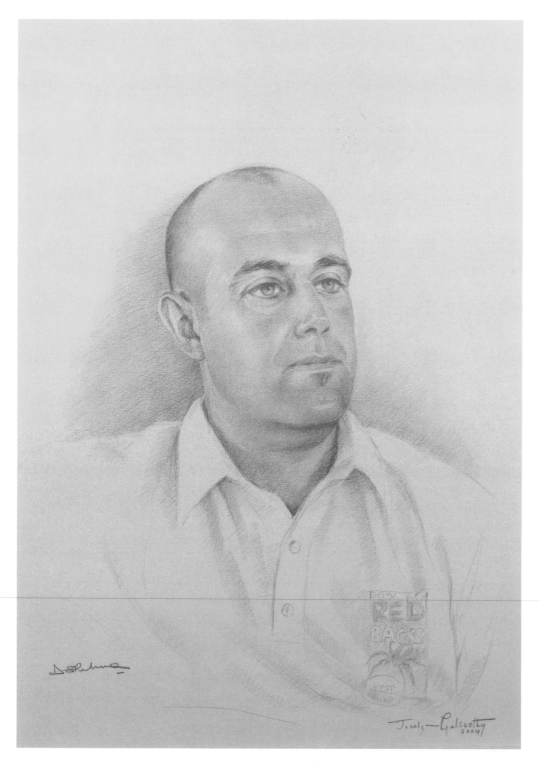

Darren Lehmann is one of those people you cannot help but like. His stocky, powerful frame and his casual, unhurried way of going, make him instantly recognisable. He has the reputation of being something of a 'larrikin' – an Aussie word with mysterious derivations – which, roughly translated, means a bit of a lad, up for most things. It may be no coincidence that one of his great friends is the actor Russell Crowe of Gladiator fame, also not unknown in larrikin circles. There is far more to Russell Crowe than meets the eye and, equally, what you see with Darren Lehmann does not accurately portray the true nature of this fine cricketer, who has had to suffer more slings and arrows than most in the course of his career. Indeed, Russell was present at David Hookes' funeral, held at the Adelaide Oval early in 2004 when Darren gave a moving farewell to his friend. David Hookes had died as the result of a tragic fall and blow to the head under circumstances which were never fully explained at the time. He had been an inspiration to the young Lehmann influencing him greatly in his love of cricket and acting as his mentor in the early years. This episode shook Darren to the core, and not only him but the rest of the team as well. They now seem to be much more protective of one another when off the field.

'Boof' as Darren is universally known, is a talented left-hand batsman who seems to have developed a style all of his own with which he can pile up the runs. He is also a useful left-arm orthodox spin bowler with the ability to take wickets at exactly the right time. His fielding can be brilliant. He started playing first class cricket at the age of 17, but did not make his Test debut, unusually, until he was 32 years old. He captains the South Australian Redbacks and plays regularly for Yorkshire and, of course, Australia. He is perceived as greatly underestimated despite his imposing record and has been overlooked too many times by the Australian selectors, but every cloud has a silver lining, so they say, and not being selected to play for his country meant that he was available to South Australia to help them win the coveted Sheffield Shield not once but twice in 1991/2 and 1995/6. Before becoming a Test cricketer, Darren had scored more first-class runs than any other Australian in the history of the game. He was an integral part of the Australian World Cup winning side of 1999 "Australia thrashes Pakistan to win Cricket World Cup", screamed the headlines – cutting medium-pace bowler Mahmood to the boundary and scoring the runs which clinched the match. He was also the catalyst behind Yorkshire's championship-winning side in 2001. Australia were again the victors in the 2003 World Cup and Darren considered the final against India to be the perfect match. He took the catch which, again, brought the Cup back to his country, thus proving his worth at the highest level.

His career has had its peaks and troughs, and it is the general consensus of opinion that he has not had an altogether fair crack of the whip. The unfortunate incident over 'racial vilification' as the authorities put it, meant much negative publicity and an ICC ban. He was suspended for five one day internationals, which may seem harsh but which reflected the seriousness with which the offence was viewed. Darren bitterly regretted the epithet in question for all that it was, supposedly, uttered in private. But walls had ears on that occasion.

During the English cricket season Darren lives in Leeds as he plays for Yorkshire with his brother-in-law, Craig (Chalky) White, the current captain. He says he is particularly partial to Leeds and its people and is always very happy when he can be there. Playing for Yorkshire can have its lighter moments. A fair amount of practical joking goes on in the dressing room in the shape of the 'Yorkshire Snipper'. This cunning individual delights in cutting off the tops of socks, jocks and ties and although Darren knows it is one of the players, he cannot work out which. The invisible snipper always targets the overseas contingent, the captain and the coach. Will he ever own up? Only time will tell. Boof, a drinking, cigarette-smoking cricketer – the last of his kind, as he puts it – has made a valiant effort to streamline his shape and become fitter. He has succeeded to a certain degree and attributes his new-found wellbeing to his busy schedule playing for Yorkshire and to Chalky's insistence on making him bowl at every opportunity.

In the Australian cricket season Darren and his wife Andrea, (who, by strange coincidence, shares his birthday) live in Adelaide with their young twins. His two older children also live in this lovely city with their mother and stepfather. As Darren is very much a family man, he has a close relationship with all his children and is also devoted to his mother. The fact that his twelve year old son made his first century for East Torrens under 14s not so long ago, pleases him greatly. He also plays golf and interests himself in his racehorse which he keeps in training in Melbourne. He is acknowledged to be a very decent man who helps the younger players, never refuses an autograph and will stop and talk to anyone who wants to talk to him. He is extremely popular with the players and the team feel that they are without doubt a more contented bunch of individuals when he is around. Darren has, recently, been recognised as *Wisden Australia's* International Cricketer of the Year on account of his inspired showing in Tests since April 2003. *Wisden Australia's* Editor was moved to comment on this accolade. "It was as if Homer Simpson had been reincarnated as Buzz Lightyear!" Boof has written his autobiography *Worth the Wait,* which he acknowledges helped him to come to terms with his friend, Hooksey's death and, perhaps, has helped him work through the frustrations of his earlier career. His attitude to the remainder of his professional life as a cricketer is nothing if not philosophical, helped in part by his success in Tests over the past eighteen months. Time is not on his side and Darren would be the first to recognise the wealth of talent waiting in the wings.

In 2004, during the Australian Tour of India, Ricky Ponting was not available for the first three Tests due to injury. Gilchrist took over as captain and Darren was made vice-captain, which must send out a strong signal about his usefulness to the team. Although, now in his 36th year, he was chosen for the 2005 One Day series in Australia. He will not be part of the Ashes Squad to visit England but he will be on hand as a commentator for BSkyB adding his talents to the likes of Ian Botham and David Gower, giving us all a unique insight, as a recent member of the team, into the workings of the Australian game.

Darren Scott Lehmann
b. 5th February 1970, Gawler, South Australia
Left-hand bat
Slow left arm orthodox

Kevin Peter Pieterson

What is 6'4", has two-tone hair which, from the front at least, looks as though he has just suffered an electric shock, exudes confidence and can bat a bit? You've guessed it – Kevin Pieterson. Kevin is another star in the making, who is absolutely determined to succeed. Born in South Africa, on the 27th June, 1980, he came from a sporting family with parents who promoted and supported him in whatever he did. "Being one of four boys, it's a free-for-all from birth", he says cheerfully and this is what has helped make him so competitive. He went to a sporting school but still managed to achieve three A-Levels in Physics, Geography and Technical Drawing. He never saw himself having a 9-5 job, and on leaving school, he began playing cricket for Natal in the 1998/99 season.

His decision to come to England, principally because he would be able to be involved in more of the sort of cricket he wanted to play, was greatly facilitated by Clive Rice, a well-respected figure in South Africa. He was influential in bringing him over to England and in introducing him to Nottingham with whom he signed a contract. He was eligible (after playing the required number of years at county cricket club level), to play for England because his mother was English. Leaving South Africa to play cricket for a rival country did not go down well in many quarters. Kevin has been subjected to scathing attacks in the press, which might have deeply affected a man of lesser character. It all seems to boil down to a loss of face because one of South Africa's assets deserted, giving the impression that, perhaps, all was not as rosy as it seemed in the South African cricket world. Kevin, himself, has undoubtedly opened his mouth a little too wide on occasions. He challenged in a hotheaded way, the crowd on the third one-day international at Port Elizabeth. Having taken a catch, he turned to the grandstand where the dark faces outnumber the white, throwing his arms up defiantly as if to say, "Yes!" By contrast, the crowd in Centurion gave him a standing ovation when on his way to collect 100 runs, he collided with Ntini and they fell to the ground in a heap. He apologised to the dazed Ntini, saluted the crowd, who to his amazement, rose to their feet and applauded him. He does not dwell on any of this, but looks forward to playing for Hampshire this season. He has signed up for three years and will be playing alongside that great Australian cricketer, Shane Warne

Since arriving in England, Kevin's skyward trajectory has seen him make his mark first for Nottinghamshire, where he had a run of big scores from the outset, earning an English Academy place and then on to a tour of Zimbabwe, where he averaged 104 in three innings. As a result of this success, he was called upon to play in the England ODI Team in South Africa in early 2005. True to form, he soon produced a century at the second ODI at Bloemfontein. The talk was centred on Kevin Pieterson, the newcomer who earned the Man of the Match and Man of the Series awards for his outstanding performances for his adopted country, in the One-Day Internationals. Ian Botham recently said of him, "He's got so much to offer the English game…in my view, England have got to pick him for the Test side. If they don't, I can see the public hanging selectors from trees." There is no doubt that he would be a tremendous asset when England face their old enemy, Australia.

For all that Kevin is an outstanding talent, he is still a very young man with a young man's fancy for fashion and Formula One. He is thrilled to have been invited to attend the Malaysian Grand Prix this year. He admits to liking to go clubbing, though is not much of a drinker. As for settling down, that will come later. He still has a lot to do and, one suspects, a certain amount of steam to let off into the bargain. This young man has a shrewd head fixed on his broad shoulders and is adamant that he will achieve his goals, whatever they may be. Oh, and he would like to make a great deal of money, too.

Kevin Peter Pieterson
b. 27th June, 1980, Pietermaritzburg, Natal, South Africa
Right hand bat
Right arm offbreak

Jason Neil Gillespie

There is no doubt that Jason Gillespie is accident-prone. This fine Australian fast bowler has had more than his fair share of injuries and niggling problems. This may have something to do with the fact that he is very tall and therefore, his back is subjected to greater stresses. He had a fluke accident when playing against Sri Lanka, colliding with Steve Waugh and suffering a broken leg and a weakened wrist. Let it never be said that Jason is faint-hearted. He has hung in there through thick and thin, totally committed and what is more, he has been given the chance to prove himself by far-seeing selectors.

Born in Sydney on 19th April, 1975, he moved to Adelaide when he was ten, where he still lives. He started watching cricket on television at about six, began playing at seven, and from the very first moment, wanted to play for Australia. At seven he was playing club cricket for Illawong in Sydney and only played school cricket when he went to live in South Australia. He played for Flagstaff Hill Primary School and joined Adelaide CC at the same time. He has two younger brothers, Rob and Luke, neither of whom have the slightest interest in the game, indeed, none of his family on either side played. This is most unusual. In fact, Jason Gillespie is a highly unusual cricketer altogether. He is part-aboriginal, the first ever to play for Australia (his father's great, great grandmother was a full-blooded Aboriginal) and he, himself is half Greek. With his long, flowing locks, he puts one in mind of Christ, or perhaps an Orthodox priest, but he is anything but priestly in the way he fires his fast balls at the opposing batsman. He says he always wanted to be a fast bowler, and he got his chance to play for his country when he was picked for his Test debut, against the West Indies, in 1996 in Sydney. The Australians won, but he had injuries. A stress fracture in his back and a strain to his side in the second Test, followed by an injury to his heel, meant that he was in and out of the team. 1n 1997, on Tour in South Africa, he took a total of 14 wickets in three Tests, followed by further injury.

Back in the side again he was bowling at his best in Kandy against Sri Lanka, when he broke his right wrist and right leg in a horrendous collision with Steve Waugh, who got off lightly with a broken nose. His next first-class game after that was in March 2000, followed by missing half the World Cup with a dodgy ankle in 2003, after playing only three games of the Tournament. He is resigned to his fate and says it is part and parcel of being a fast bowler and something you just have to get used to. Fingers crossed, he appears to be on song again. He has shortened his run-up and varied the pace to a greater extent then before. His batting has been improving steadily and he can now be relied upon to hold his own and significantly increase the score at the tail-end, which is extremely valuable to the side.

What does Jason get up to when he is not playing cricket or lying in a hospital bed? He is married to Anna, (they tied the knot on a boat, barefoot and totally informally) in Port Douglas, Queensland the year before last, 2003 and he is building a house in the eastern suburbs, about four kilometres from the Adelaide Oval. His new wife tends to travel with him, whenever possible, while the going is good. He has a daughter with the very pretty name of Sapphire, whom he sees as much as possible. He is trying to put a few ideas in place for the future when he leaves cricket altogether, although it doesn't bear thinking about as he is still in love with the game. If he chose to stay around cricket, which is not certain, he would want to do something to help young people entering the game. He has talked about having his own radio show with Damien Fleming; 'a bit of sport, a bit of music (his kind – hard rock) and a bit of a laugh.' He would love to play basketball as a social sport only. He certainly has the height, but could he stand the pace? He does not have any plans to write a book until the end of his career, but he has been mentioned in Matt Hayden's cookery book as the man who recommended the best food in the world, 'Bangers and Mash'.

Not unnaturally, Jason is very interested in Aboriginal rights and culture. He says with conviction that the Aboriginal culture is truly fantastic and he wants to see it promoted. So far as sport goes, he has held coaching clinics for aboriginals on the Torre Strait islands on behalf of Cricket Australia, which he has thoroughly enjoyed.

He is also the Chief Executive Officer for Aboriginal Rights in South Australia.

Jason has a nickname, 'Dizzy', but he wishes to inform everyone that he plays the saxophone, not the trumpet! In his autobiography, Shane Warne pays tribute to Dizzy. "He is an inspiration to kids everywhere for his courage: another of the good guys in the game. He works hard and does some funny things... has a good sense of humour and is always looking for something to make us laugh."

He will be part of the Ashes Squad and if he is his old self, we are in for a treat and a half. The Aussie line-up of fast bowlers will be formidable, no doubt, but whatever the outcome, the 'good guy' Jason Dizzy Gillespie, a top quality bowler, will be giving it his all.

Jason Neil Gillespie
b. 19th April, 1975, Darlinghurst, Sydney, NSW, Australia
Right hand bat
Right arm fast

Muttiah Muralitharan

ri Lankan superstar of the cricket world, highly accomplished offspinner and exponent of the controversial, but oh so effective doosra, Muttiah 'Murali' Muralitharan, is one of the two most exciting bowlers in the world today. Along with Shane Warne, this man dominates the bowling wherever he plays. He was educated at a strict boarding school in Kandy, played cricket and was a medium pace bowler to begin with. He was persuaded to try his hand at off-cutters when the school team were short of a slow bowler. From the word go, he had the ability to turn the ball and very soon his wicket-taking exploits were being written up in the newspapers. He was encouraged by his father, a biscuit manufacturer and his mother who adored cricket to further his career in Colombo. In 1991, he toured England and nearly gave cricket up altogether as he had not taken a single wicket in three first-class games. However, the Sri Lankan captain, Arjuna Ranatunga, who became his mentor believed in Murali's potential as a bowler and fast-tracked him into the side.

In 1992, Murali joined the Test team and, from the outset, his strange bowling action provoked controversy, which instead of dying down, flared up into an international row, culminating in a ruling by the ICC. Murali is a private and modest man, totally professional in public with a more relaxed side on show when he is with friends. He plays for Lancashire as well as for Sri Lanka and on arriving in Manchester recently, expressed his relief at being alive after narrowly missing the Tsunami which devastated so much of his island on Boxing Day. On a tour of the devastated areas he was so shocked at the destruction, he decided to set up a house-building programme. Twenty-five houses have already been built in Galle, home to a lovely cricket ground. This is an ongoing project and one which he is determined to see through. He is also an Ambassador for the United Nations Food Programme, joining the campaign to feed the world's hungry children. Shane Warne promised to help in the task of reconstruction through his own Foundation and the City of Melbourne, having a soft spot for Sri Lanka and Galle where he took his 500th Test wicket. The two best bowlers in the world, deadly rivals on the field, have come together to help a cause bigger than both of them and are to be admired for the contribution they are making. Murali has reservations, though, about the rich nations, who gave so much towards the rebuilding of devastated areas, actually delivering what has been promised. Progress is so slow and people are still so traumatised that if donations are to do any good, they must get through and quickly.

Murali's debut in ODIs came in 1993 against India at Colombo. And he has gone on to net 366 ODI wickets as well as 532 Test wickets. His biggest battle now is with his fitness – those injuries to which all bowlers are prey, but in Murali's case he has had to undergo a shoulder operation not long ago, but should be back on form for the coming season playing for Lancashire. He has, at last, found the perfect companion in Madhi Ramamurthy, whom he married in March in a symbolic and beautiful South Indian ceremony. She is a business studies graduate and the Director of a leading heart hospital founded by her late father, but on her wedding day, radiant in the traditional red sari with heavy gold embroidery, she could have been an Indian bride from any age in history as she demurely followed her husband in the rites of this ancient ceremony. She says she knew nothing about cricket at first, but has tried to learn and will do as much as she can to support him in his desire to keep on playing for as long as he can.

The strange bowling action which is such a feature of Murali's deliveries has been heavily criticised and minutely examined. Murali is double-jointed which gives him an advantage straight away when it comes to turning the ball and apparently, he was born with a certain congenital deformity which prevents his arm from straightening fully. He also has a structural imbalance in his pelvis, though no-one is suggesting that this has anything to do with the matter of his arm action. Some 'experts' say he throws the ball, notably the umpire Darrell Hair, and this debate carries on, despite Murali's exoneration by the ICC and various medical opinions. Mark Nicholas devised a test for him, on television, to prove the case one way or the other by encasing his arm in a cast and getting him to bowl his trademark doosra. Mark, former successful captain of Hampshire and now working for Channel Four, could see nothing wrong with Murali's action at all. Even Shane Warne has come down on his side, telling the press that Murali is not a chucker. Before this wizard with the ball moved centre stage, his style of bowling had only been seen by Saqlain Mushtaq, the inventor of the doosra. The ball can be rotated using the fingers or the wrist, but never before had a bowler rotated his whole hand and no-one could quite believe the crescendo of the Muralitharan fast spin. A lesser man might have been severely affected by

all the criticism he has had to suffer. However, this mesmerising man from Sri Lanka shows no bitterness, hiding behind his smile and not revealing the anguish he must, at times, have felt. Hopefully, he can put it all behind him and concentrate on remaining fully fit for the coming season, when he will delight the crowds with his bowling and shine once more in the cricket arena like the star he has become.

Muttiah Muralitharan
b. 17th April, Kandy, Sri Lanka
Right hand bat
Right arm off-spin
One of *Wisden's* Five Cricketers of the Year, 1999
Lancashire Player of the Year, 1999
Highest wicket-taker in Test Cricket, 2000 and 2001
Several Man of the Match Awards

Andrew Flintoff

Big is beautiful and they don't come much bigger than the blonde good-looking Andrew (Freddie) Flintoff. It isn't all skin-deep, either, this baby-faced cricketer from the North can really play. Hailed as the new Ian Botham, he had a reputation to live up to before he ever joined the England team, which was patently unfair. However, Freddie did give the crowds something to watch, as Ian had done, biffing the ball all round the ground, creating unbearable tension when one thought things might go wrong and he might self-destruct. His health problems have been much publicised, the latest of these being the operation to his ankle, which has been done early enough for him to be fighting fit for the 2005 Ashes series.

Born in Preston, Lancashire, on 6th December, 1977, he was allowed to do his own thing to a great extent when playing cricket. His father never made him bat or bowl in a certain way and his coaching was kept to a minimum. He just hit and hit anything that came his way. Having an older brother, Chris, was good for him he says, as it kept him up to the mark, striving to keep pace with him. He probably always wanted to play cricket for a living, but when the careers adviser saw that he had written 'professional cricketer' in answer to the question of his future occupation, he told him to think of a more realistic option! Luckily for Lancashire and England, Freddie ignored this advice.

Andrew Flintoff joined several under-19 Tours to the West Indies, Zimbabwe and Pakistan, then in 1997/8 an England A team Tour to Kenya and Sri Lanka. In 1998 he made his Test debut, England against South Africa at Trent Bridge and complained that he felt ignored and marginalised by the other members of the team who hardly spoke to him. He only managed to make 17 runs on that occasion. In July 2000, he was Man of the Match at the England v Zimbabwe match at Old Trafford. He was having a hard time from the press who were told he was overweight (this, supposedly, from the England management) and his quick remark to them after his award was, "Not bad for a fat lad". In July of the same year, playing in the NatWest Trophy quarter final for Lancashire against Surrey at the Oval, he was 135 not out from 111 balls and Lancashire won by eight wickets with fourteen overs to spare.

By September 2001, at the end of an unlucky season, Andrew asked Duncan Fletcher if he could attend the ECB National Academy in Adelaide. This seems to have done the trick and given him a whole new outlook. While he was in Adelaide the call came for him to join the England side in their match against India at Bangalore. His batting was disappointing against the Indian spinners, but he more than made up for this with his bowling. Using a technique more suited to the bodyline era, he sent the ball straight at Tendulkar's ribs and proceeded to repeat the exercise with other batsmen until he ended up with 9 for 28 and 4 for 50, helping England to secure a first innings lead of 98, until rain intervened. Again he was voted Man of the Match. Another memorable match for him, England against India in Mumbai, January, 2002, saw him bowl Javagal Srinath off the penultimate ball to tie the six-match one-day series. Andrew was so elated at what he had just done that he yanked off his shirt in delight. "I tend to get excited when I take a wicket, especially in India", he says by way of excuse. It took a long time, but it was worth it when he made his maiden Test hundred in an England v New Zealand match at Christchurch. He made his hundred in true 'Beefy' fashion, off 114 balls, hooking it over the keeper's head. Andrew was flying when, suddenly, most likely because he had been playing for far too long, he developed a hernia which put paid to things until July 2003. From that date until the end of July, 2004 he captured 12 one-day international wickets from 12 matches. When batting, he scored 551 runs in these 12 matches at an average of 78.71. As a result he was named ODI Player of the Year at the ICC Awards held in London, in September, 2004. That year, England had won 11 and drawn 2 of its 13 Tests. A revitalised Andrew Flintoff had played no small part in this achievement. Andrew's ankle started playing up again during the Tour to South Africa in 2004/5, but he soldiered on, bowling better than he batted and ended up top of the bowling averages for the series. He was sent home to have the operation he needed, the operation which the England team all hope will see him back in action with a vengeance for the Ashes in 2005.

Freddie is extremely modest about his achievements. "I just play the game as I enjoy playing it and it seems to work", he says. There seems to be no conscious effort to be a crowd-pleaser, but even he must realise that there is such a thing as the Flintoff factor. This draws the crowds and keeps them on the edge of their seats on occasions. He is very generous to players who drop him; he just smiles and says it could happen to anyone. He is bighearted, humorous and a most endearing, if somewhat chaotic, individual. His disregard for the conventions of batting, such as playing yourself in and not taking risks at the start of your innings, means that he starts with a bang, usually hitting a boundary within the first ten balls. He is physically very powerful and hitting hard comes naturally. He is reminiscent to a certain degree of another hard-hitting batsman, whose lack of inhibition at the crease sometimes scared the bowlers witless. They never knew quite whether they were safe, even if they ducked. Freddie has recently married and feels that his life is much more stable now. He is happy in himself, except that sleep (one of his favourite pastimes) is a little harder to come by these days as he has a toddler to keep up with.

According to people who have tried to coach him, Freddie has worked hard to tighten up his game and curb his enthusiasm when called for. He has wanted to practice his batting skills on a daily basis, skills which will allow him to show his natural talent, but at the same time, fend off the dangers, keeping him in for as long as possible. This very likeable, good tempered, highly talented all-rounder is now poised for a new and exciting season when he will be called upon, as never before, to prove himself against the most formidable side in the world. We all wait, with mounting anticipation, to witness the Flintoff factor at work.

Andrew Flintoff
b. 6th December, Preston, Lancashire, England
Right hand bat
Right arm fast medium

Henry Khaaba Olonga

Tall, dark and handsome Henry Olonga, former Zimbabwean fast bowler does not lack for courage. He stood up to be counted, together with his captain and fellow cricketer Andy Flower, a gesture which cost him his career and his homeland. When Andy approached Henry about taking a stand against the Mugabe government, he made the point that normal sport in an abnormal society simply does not work. The government would fasten on the World Cup to demonstrate that all was well with Zimbabwe and, clearly all was far from well. The two men wore black armbands at the opening game of the World Cup in Harare in 2003, to mourn 'the death of democracy' under the despotic regime of Robert Mugabe. It was a brave thing to have done, particularly for a black cricketer, and while many in Zimbabwe disagreed with it or failed to understand the protest, the English-speaking cricketing fraternity admired the bravery and moral conviction of both Henry and Andy. That admiration remains undiminished two years on, although much has changed in the lives of both the protestors since then. Unlike Andy, Henry did not have an English club ready to sign him and he was undecided as to what he was going to do. To add insult to injury, his girlfriend of three years' standing e-mailed him to say that their relationship was over. No wonder – Robert Mugabe's brother was her grandfather.

Music has always played a very important role in his life and with his fine voice, he contemplated singing, perhaps R&B, perhaps even opera if he could get the backing he needed. Henry had recorded a single entitled 'Our Zimbabwe' in which he tried to say that his country did not belong exclusively to either black or white. It reached the top of the local charts, demonstrating that people wanted to listen to his voice and that, maybe, a professional career as a singer would be open to him. This thought must have sustained him as he contemplated what seemed to be a bleak future. No more cricket for his country. No more visits to his homeland.

Henry is a remarkable young man. He is extremely eloquent and has travelled around England singing and speaking and even coaching schoolboys. He has given interviews and fielded questions in a manner worthy of a politician and in doing so, has collected a coterie of admirers. Nevertheless, as a young man, on his own and away from his family who are scattered round the globe, life must have seemed unbearable at times. In 2004 he returned to Africa to see his father, a paediatrician in Bulawayo, but they were compelled by the situation to meet in Kenya. Henry's mother lives in Australia where she works as a nurse and there was speculation that Henry might live in that country. He had an Australian friend, Tara Read whom he met several years ago and with whom he kept in touch. Their friendship blossomed into romance and Henry asked her to marry him. Needless to say, Andy Flower was one of the first to congratulate him on his good taste and good fortune. For the moment, Henry is living in Middlesex until his nationality problems are resolved. He is concentrating on music, after-dinner speaking and his newly rekindled interest in painting. He reflects that, even when he was playing cricket, he always felt there was something missing. He needed to have an occupation which would be deeply satisfying on more than one level and he has found this satisfaction in painting. Being traditional in his approach to art, he concentrates mainly on portraits and animal subjects. He acknowledges Jocelyn Galsworthy as being one of the influences which have inspired him to take up his pencils and brushes once more.

It must seem a long time ago that Henry, aged 19, became the first black cricketer and the youngest-ever player to represent Zimbabwe. At the age of 17 he made his first-class debut in the Logan Cup for Mashonaland. Full of hope and full of promise he set about turning himself into a pace bowler, not without difficulty and he called upon Dennis Lillee to help him sort out his action. In 1998 he took five wickets against India at the Harare Sports Club and in 2000 *six wickets for 19 runs* at Newlands against England. He is proud to have bowled to most of the top batsmen in the world including Sachin Tendulkar and to have faced Wasim Akram. Henry's international career is now over, but he sees a bigger picture and does not regret for one minute the protest he made. Following that fateful day, he has been hounded by the Zimbabwe police, forced to seek refuge in South Africa and has ended up in England, with trips to Australia, a country he likes and admires. They, in turn, honour the stance he has taken. The sentence for treason in Zimbabwe is death and it is unlikely that Henry will be going home in the near future. He did what he did for the people of his country and he is enormously grateful to all those who have shown understanding and

compassion for their suffering. Change will come, he is sure of that and this thought sustains him. This dignified man has earned the respect of the world and there cannot be many people who have never heard the name Henry Olonga.

Henry Khaaba Olonga
b. 3rd July, 1976, Lusaka, Namibia
Right hand bat
Right arm fast
Commentator

Matthew Peter Maynard

Approaching 40, with a Testimonial season to look forward to, and a new career as Assistant coach to Duncan Fletcher and the England side, Matthew Maynard seems to be erring, for once, on the side of caution. Nicknamed 'Ollie' (after the late Oliver Reed), Matthew was an exciting man with a bat, a big talent with a big future.

Born in Oldham, Lancashire on 21st March, 1966, cricket came into his life through his father, who played as a semi professional cricketer in the Lancashire Leagues, after a professional boxing career of 66 fights, retiring at the age of 27. Matthew remembers that he and his brother used to watch the Aston Nomads play when they were growing up and used to have a knock around at the same time. Matthew used to watch all the fights as well and took a very keen interest in Muhammed Ali, collecting memorabilia avidly over the years. At 14 he realised that he wanted to play cricket professionally, but felt that if it failed to work out, he could always run a pub like his parents, who kept one at Menai Bridge in Anglesey. It was a good trade to be in as one did not have to work all day, every day and the profits were reasonable. He went to school in Wales, where most of the conversation was in Welsh, but how much he has retained of the language is difficult to say. He had wanted to play rugby for the Scarlets in

Llanelli, but a neck injury, suffered while playing in the schoolboy under-15s final precluded him from doing so and he never played rugby again.

He first played cricket for the school at Menai Bridge cricket club when he was eleven, keeping wicket and batting. It was left to his brother Charlie to bowl. His father felt that he needed to play a better standard of cricket and he went to Bangor cricket club, where he was coached by Bill Clutterbuck. This man had a huge influence on Matthew's playing career. He would throw and bowl to him in the nets for hours and in return, Matthew helped him with the ground at Bangor. At 15, playing in an end of season match there, Chairman's Team against the First Eleven, batting first, he was 20 not out by lunch. He downed a couple of beers and some wine and, feeling mellow, he 'smacked' the bowlers round the ground for a century. Colin Page at Kent CCC came to hear of it, and that is how he ended up, at 16, in 1982, playing for Kent for two and a half years. Midway through 1984, Glamorgan were showing an interest and he went for a trial, did well and was offered a contract for the 1985 season. It was a great sadness to Matthew that his father died shortly after he heard the news and was never able to see him play a first-class game. Matthew has stuck with the county ever since and became captain in 1992 in Alan Butcher's absence and then again in 1996 until the end of the 2000 season. He had come a long way since the early days at Glamorgan, when he admits they were a poor side incapable of winning. With four one-day titles, a championship and a Lord's final to their credit, no-one can say that now.

He became the youngest player to be capped by Glamorgan and in 1988 was voted Young Cricketer of the Year. Previously, he had become the youngest ever Glamorgan player to score 1000 runs. His debut for England came in 1988 against the West Indies at the Oval, when the England Selectors could no longer ignore this up and coming young talent. Two years before these honours came his way, he married Sue, at the tender age of twenty, and this may well have coloured his thinking when he decided to join Mike Gatting's rebel tour to South Africa. As a young, professional sportsman, now with a wife, he decided to earn some money for the future without thinking through what he was doing and without understanding the situation in South Africa. Viv Richards had by now been signed up to play for Glamorgan and Matthew (or perhaps Ollie, more appropriately), became fast friends with Viv and 'Beefy' and has helped the latter on his charity walks which he enjoys immensely, especially when it is benefiting such wonderful causes as the Noah's

Ark Hospital in Cardiff. Through Lord's Taverners, he has organised matches in Cardiff and is always ready to help on the charitable front in any way he can.

Matthew Maynard is a thoroughly engaging individual. He is England's answer to Andy Flower in the Action Man stakes, never standing still for a minute, always off doing something dangerous or headstrong, but remains incredibly loyal to the club which first signed him up and for which he has done such service. His international career, or lack of it, was a keenly-felt disappointment. The Selectors seemed unable to make up their minds about him and stick with him to give him the best chance of succeeding. In 1988, he says, he was the 29th person to be used in that Test series.

All that is history and he looks forward immensely to proving himself in his new role of Assistant Coach. Duncan Fletcher has brought stability to the England team and they are now playing a whole lot better, in his opinion. Not only is this his opinion. If England can keep it together, and if the media roots for them instead of piling on the pressure which has a negative effect, then there might be a chance against the Aussies. To come back from South Africa having won the series 2-1 was a terrific achievement. Did the media think so? Hell no. Matthew is nothing if not forthright. He admits to taking each day as it comes as he is an instinctive type of person. If something is right, then he will go with it wholeheartedly. His father had two sayings: 'Live every day as if it is your last, because one day you'll be right' and 'Never go to bed the same day as you got up'. He is pretty good at following both those bits of advice, admitting that he has had a great life so far, although he has had to tone it down a little! As a responsible father of two, Tom (on tour with the England under-16s) and Ceri, 11, who enjoys playing football, doing gymnastics and horse riding (and probably looks like her dear old Dad, as well), he has to think of their future in addition to his own. He begins a new chapter in a career that has had its superlative moments and one thing is certain, he will give it 100 per cent and his dedication to the job will be second to none.

Matthew Peter Maynard
b. 21st March, 1966, Oldham, Lancashire, England
Right Hand bat
Right Arm Medium
Wicketkeeper

Two worst moments of his career:
Bowled out by Bazalgette at 'The Bat and Ball'
Bowled out by a girl

Darren Gough

'Dazzler', the Yorkshire, Essex and England fast bowler is one of the best known and best loved cricketers on the scene in recent years. Born near Barnsley in Yorkshire on 18th September, 1970, his first love had been football and not cricket. It was a great disappointment to him when he found out he was not really good enough to make it his profession. That left cricket. He joined Barnsley cricket club and worked at the Indoor School at Headingley, as part of a YTS initiative. In 1989, he was put on the Yorkshire staff, spending most of his time at the Cricket Academy, either with a paint brush in his hand or a broom, getting the place ready for the grand opening. He couldn't play because of a back problem (possibly caused by being overweight – 'Guzzler' was his nickname in those days) so was chosen to receive the ceremonial first ball, bowled by Bob Appleyard, a legend in Yorkshire. Unfortunately, Darren didn't know that, and determined to show off, hit the ball for six, over the bemused Bob Appleyard's head, simply because he could not help himself. It is easy to imagine the talking-to he got for that.

Coming to London, to play at Lord's against Middlesex for the first time, is something he will never forget. Merely walking through the Grace Gates into the visitors' dressing room and out on to the hallowed turf almost reduced him to tears, it was so exciting and emotional. The same thing happened to him on his England debut. He got lucky and very soon had his first wicket, none other than the Middlesex captain Mike Gatting's, in a first-class match. Darren had bagged five wickets on his debut and was mentioned in all the newspapers. He was the first YTS boy to play for his county and now earned more money than he could have dreamed of when he first started out. It was at this point that he knew he wanted to make cricket his life.

His back problems began in earnest when he was required to bowl thirteen consecutive overs, a crazy thing to do to a youngster, and his back suffered to the extent that he had to stop bowling altogether, for a while. Ironically, the fact that he had an enforced bowling lay-off, helped his batting greatly. Darren certainly had the temperament to cope with the big time. He was nobody's fool and stood up for himself, giving as good as he got and not letting the pressure get to him. His under-19 tour of Australia went well, but at Yorkshire things were unsettled. Falling revenue and die-hard decisions were depressing everyone. Suddenly, it was decided to scrap the Yorkshire-born policy and allow in players who merely lived in the county. This gave everyone a fillip and Darren made a good showing when next he played at Headingley, impressing Derek Shackleton, who wrote him a letter thanking him for his hard work. Pretty soon 'Guzzler' had become 'Dazzler'. He received his cap (though not before being upset at the insensitive way it had been handled) and turned down a much more lucrative offer to play for Northants. He was sticking with Yorkshire. Darren felt that 1994 might be his year, particularly as the Yorkshireman Ray Illingworth was now Chairman of Selectors. Sure enough, he was selected to play for England, the one thing he had longed for and which he had dreamt about for years. It did not take long before the media started in on him: 'Gough the Scoff – I was a Yorkshire Pudding' read one headline. However, Anna, his wife, had helped him slim down and shape up and he did not mind this banter. He was at heart a bit of a showoff and quite tough enough to deal with this sort of thing. As long as Yorkshire politics stayed out of the equation, he was happy. After the one-day international in 1994, where he took 2 wickets, including Martin Crowe's, he was hailed as England's new fast bowling sensation. Martin Crowe congratulated him and gave him his shirt, which pleased him but not nearly as much as his wicket. His first Lord's Test did not go well. The new South Africa were determined to win and England, it seemed, were determined to shoot themselves in the foot. The famous incident with dirt being rubbed onto the ball by Atherton, led to heavy handed reprisals (in the middle of the match), which destroyed concentration and gave England very little chance of making a comeback. Far better to have dealt with it afterwards. Allan Donald, the South African fast bowler, had inflicted damage on Darren's arm, mercifully not broken, but he was off for a while. He wrote on a piece of paper in the dressing room, 'Donald Dies', which the media fastened on, knowing full well that it was only a figure of speech. Revenge never was exacted, though Darren did try. He certainly did not feel like turning up for the regulation photograph taken with the grinning South African Team. His arm hurt too much for that.

Dazzler's greatest triumph must, surely, be the time he performed the hat trick in front of a massive Australian crowd at the SCG on the 1998/99 Ashes Tour. The Aussie batting had been inspired up to that point, then Dazzler

struck with all his might and skill, taking three wickets in as many balls (the last time this had been done in an Ashes Series was at Headingley in 1899). However, Darren's efforts were to no avail on this occasion. The previous Test, in Melbourne on Boxing Day saw England stage a remarkable recovery when Headley and Gough turned the tables on Australia on the fourth day. Ramprakash held a spectacular catch in the slips which set off the Australian demise. Darren had seven catches dropped off his bowling in the same 1998 series affecting his confidence and, consequently, his bowling performance. This time, England won, much to the amazement of the Australians, who had left the ground and were heading home, only to hear the news on their radios. Darren is very well-liked in Australia and he reciprocates. They are generous to their opponents off the field, hospitable and friendly, which makes a deal of difference when you are far from home. Darren's

thrilling catch on the boundary at Lord's in 2000 decided the outcome of the Test match v the West Indies, when they were bowled out for 56 and finally lost to England for the first time in 31 years. Dazzler was Man of the Series that summer. In the 2005 South African ODI series he was named the bowler with the best performance, quite an achievement at 34 with a dodgy knee.

Darren 'Dazzler' Gough has been a wonderful servant both to his country and his county (which he left in 2004 to play for Essex). He is an enthusiastic, outgoing character, who does not mince his words and who does not like injustice (just ask Devon Malcolm). He is a great fan of Lord MacLaurin and it is his opinion that English cricket would be in dire straits now if it were not for Lord MacLaurin's time at the ECB. He is a showman, he loves interacting with the crowd and his natural good manners and air of confidence make him instantly likeable. He does not believe in crushing someone's spirit to make them conform and is always willing to impart his experience to the younger players. He has two wonderful boys, Liam and Brennan and is a devoted family man. This talented fast bowler is a marvellous role model, who from humble beginnings has made it to the very top of is game. He has delighted crowds all over the world and has endeared himself to everyone with his bright smile and unfailing cheerfulness, no matter how dire the situation. His attitude, commitment and determination have brought him one of his goals – to get 200 Test wickets. His second wish will, now, never be fulfilled. He wanted to be part of an England team to win the Ashes. While he cannot be a team member, he might be in the front row, watching an England win sooner than he thinks.

Darren Gough
b. 18th September, 1970, Barnsley, Yorkshire
Right hand bat
Right arm fast

Yorkshire Sports Personality of the Year, 1994
Cornhill England Player of the Year 1994/5 and 1998/9
One of *Wisden's* Five Cricketers of the Year 1999
Freeserve Fast Ball Award 2000 (93.1 mph at Lord's)
Vodafone England Cricketer of the Year 2000/1
Several Man of the Match and Man of the Series Awards

THE STEWARD &
THE GROUNDSMAN

Eric Bernard Dawson

Eric Dawson has a feather in his cap, a red, tyrolean-sort of a feather which bristles up from his trademark panama, announcing to everyone that he is on hand, ready to smooth the way for all those visiting the Mound Stand at Lord's where, as supervisor, he reigns supreme.

Born in Jamaica, he was, he says with some regret, expelled from the technical college he attended and sent to England to be 'sorted out' by his older sister, who had lived in the country since 1948. Before coming to England, he spent a few months with another sister in Brooklyn, New York, but the pace of life did not suit one used to the languid, comfortable Jamaican rhythms and he made the journey to England, finally, in 1952. Within nine months of landing, he was summoned to do his National Service, which he spent most enjoyably in the RAF. He played cricket for his squadron, and did so well that he was invited to play county cricket.

Eric's love of the game began in Jamaica where he was drawn into it by the great George Headley, whose son played for the West Indies and his grandson for England. The radio provided Eric with the excitement he needed to fuel his enthusiasm and, at the age of 7, he was taken to watch his very first game. From that moment on, he was hooked. George Headley became his hero and he made sure he went to every match in which the great man was playing. The young Eric was extremely fortunate to have been coached by Headley, at a cricket club formed for underprivileged children and sponsored by local businesses. As well as cricket coaching, there were general classes to encourage education. One lesson Eric will never forget, was when he was bowling to a youngster who played a bad stroke. George Headley asked Eric to bowl slowly so that the boy could correct his previous stroke. Instead of a slow ball, Eric, who by now was getting good at the game, and fancied himself as a spin bowler, let rip with the ball and bowled the youngster out. The coach was not amused. He told Eric that the first thing he must learn was to obey the captain. This sticks in his mind, even now, and has probably, subconsciously, influenced him all his life.

Certainly, it is hard to imagine Eric putting a foot wrong. His whole approach to life and work seems to have been to try to do his very best at all times to lighten the load of others in whatever way he can. For this reason, he is much loved and greatly respected by all at Lord's, where he has worked first part-time, then full-time, for 40 years. To begin with Eric worked only on Saturday, Monday and Tuesday, the rest of the week being spent at an engineering company in Ealing. When the Glacier Metal Company ceased to trade and Eric was made redundant, he was instantly snapped up by Lord's.

His job as supervisor of the Mound Stand entails briefing 179 men on match days, delegating tasks, meeting and greeting the good and the great – "nice people, beautiful people", he smiles – and generally going out of his way to be helpful. One of the stories Eric tells to illustrate this fact is about the lady with the young baby who was howling lustily and creating quite a disturbance. Since there were several empty boxes in the Mound Stand on that particular day, he invited the young lady to watch the cricket from one of them, thus pleasing her and, at the same time, keeping the yelling baby out of earshot. But his task was not yet done. In her haste the young mother had forgotten a vital piece of baby equipment. Guess who drove all round the area hunting for nappies? This act of kindness has never been forgotten. The lady wrote to the Secretary, then Colonel John Stephenson, praising the Mound Stand supervisor. Eric felt proud to have been singled out in this way and Colonel Stephenson was equally gratified to know that the reputation of MCC was enhanced by his wonderful staff. Eric admits that he tries to set a high standard and this does not go unnoticed by the many VIPs he has to deal with. Some, like the late Sir Paul Getty, were great friends. On a visit to Wormsley, Eric was pleased and flattered to be taken to the library and shown a book which had cost £4 million pounds. Sir Paul also marked his fortieth birthday by sending him a case of champagne. John Major was a friend who, when he was Chancellor, offered to help Eric over a puzzling financial matter...in return for Eric's best endeavours to persuade Norma to watch a cricket match. He failed. The great Australian cricketers such as the Chappell brothers, Neil Harvey and Keith Miller always remembered and greeted him and Lord MacLaurin, former Chairman of the ECB, always refers to him as The Governor. When he was Chairman of Tesco, Lord MacLaurin once commandeered a box in the Mound Stand without telling Eric. He apologised profusely and gave him fifty pounds' worth of Tesco vouchers. This must have pleased Eric, or more probably, Phyllis his wife, very much indeed. "Phyllis", he says, "is my soul mate". They met as youngsters in Jamaica and were so suited to each other in every way that Miss Dawkins soon became Mrs Dawson, much to the delight of both families to whom they remain very close.

The Members at Lord's have been extremely generous to Eric and Phyllis. When Phyllis was in hospital, Eric was presented with a 'get well' card, large enough to accommodate 979 signatures, and a bouquet of flowers to give her at the next visit. Phyllis was so overcome by such thoughtfulness that she burst into tears. When she was better, she came to Lord's and was soundly hugged by everybody she saw. It is such special treatment which makes Eric so proud to be a part of this unique club. Only on rare occasions has Eric experienced unpleasantness from members in the course of his duties, but the gratitude and praise he gets, and richly deserves, far outweigh any lapses on the part of the membership.

Eric is universally held in high esteem and now that he has retired, so that he can better look after his wife, sadly wheelchair-bound, Lord's will never be quite the same again.

Eric Bernard Dawson

Michael John Hunt

ick Hunt is the cheery, laid-back character who is Head Groundsman at Lord's, ultimately responsible for the condition of the ground when it comes to cricket, particularly Test cricket, every year. He was born in London on 5th June, 1952, and as a young boy, loved going to watch his father play club cricket every Sunday in the summer months. As a child, Mick also played cricket, at school, where one season, he captained the first side. He was very keen on football as well as cricket and was always to be found hitting or kicking a ball during the holidays

Mick was an apprentice electrician for a while after leaving school, but could not settle to an indoor job. He much preferred being outside. As luck would have it, his father knew Ted Swannell, Head Groundsman at Lord's in those days, who said there was a vacancy, which in 1969 Mick was able to fill. When he first started, the job consisted mainly of fetching and carrying, but Mick gradually worked his way up to using machinery. After a while, Jim Fairbrother from Trent Bridge took over Ted's job.

At the end of the cricket season, the grass has to recover and the laborious task of preparing for the new season the following year begins. The grass is still growing up to early November, and when the really cold weather comes, that is the time to move inside and overhaul and maintain the equipment. There is a tremendous feeling of satisfaction on the eve of a match, when the grass looks stunning – a brilliant emerald green, beautifully manicured with its finishing touch of chequered pattern. The pitch is as near perfect as one can make it. After a match, the ground is irrigated and given a feed to perk it up. At the end of the season, of course, it is reseeded with rye grass and given a light covering of soil. Luckily, Lord's does not suffer from moles, but there is a fox, which is starting to become a nuisance, digging for worms. Urban foxes are now suffering from a diminishing supply of food, as people are using wheelie bins for their rubbish which the fox finds impossible to penetrate. Black sacks full of leftovers are being discouraged and the ready supply of snacks to which they had been accustomed is now being cut off. Will Mick Hunt have to turn hunter if the fox gets too annoying?

On the whole, the visitors to Lord's are very well-behaved, but Mick does see the odd tearaway, who has had too much to drink walking onto the pitch. He also finds bread rolls and bottles on his carefully nurtured greensward. Some even try to dig up a bit of turf as a souvenir. Mick remembers being horrified at the South African team, some of whom marked the pitch with gouged-out crosses. He had never seen anything like it before and hopes never to see it again. Then, of course,

there are the streakers. They mostly come from the Nursery end gap. One gets an inkling it is going to happen, he says. If it's a woman, she is encouraged by the crowd, if a man, there are shouts of "Get him off, cover him up", particularly if he is well-endowed! Most people are in awe of the place, though, especially those who take tours round Lord's. It is still a cricket ground as opposed to the stadium it would become if ever Lord's lost its trees.

Sometimes captains ask his opinion as to whether to bat or field when they win the toss. On one occasion, he advised a captain of India to field and put England in to bat. England went on to score more than 600 runs. Needless to say, the Indian captain was none too pleased. Mick gets on very well with the New Zealand team in particular and he has been to both New Zealand and Australia on his travels. He was even asked to look at a proposed cricket ground in Spain which ex-pats wanted to develop. It was on a marvellously picturesque site facing the sea with mountains behind. Nothing has come of it, unfortunately. According to Mick, because the game is now so pressurised, everyone is terribly serious all the time and the fun seems to have gone out of it. By contrast, Colin Ingleby-MacKenzie, who knew all about fun when he was playing, held a birthday bash not long ago in the Media Centre at Lord's, which ended in a firework display. A thumping great lorry arrived, and the ensuing display was very noisy indeed. Mick describes the din as "horrendous". Beforehand, Colin had cheerfully informed Mick that there would only be "a couple of bangs!" It must be very worrying for him when he ends up at the sharp end of the complaints and he says it is no fun at all when the press make unfounded criticism about the pitches he has taken so much time and trouble to prepare to the best of his ability.

Lord's has a splendid new, computerised irrigation system. This has greatly helped matters because the system before could only be used during the day as it had to be moved around to cover all parts. The water merely evaporated during the day and did no good at all. The new system is timed and computerised, which can catch people out if they decide to take a short cut across the ground. They get soaked.

Mick is married to an Irish wife, Rose, who is a nurse at the Wellington hospital in St. John's Wood, which is highly convenient for Lord's. They were married in South Armagh in 1974 and had to be chaperoned everywhere because of the situation in Northern Ireland. They have a house in Ireland to which they might retire when the time comes. He is a father and grandfather. His eldest son, Kieran, was an excellent rugby player and played for the Saracens. He has a degree in Sports Psychology which is all the rage at the moment. He also has two daughters, and says that he is now financially scarred for life as they both got married recently, one to a cricketer. The other daughter held her reception at the Finchley Cricket Club.

Lord's is difficult to maintain because of the amount of fixtures and the size of the square, which has an excessive amount of wear and tear. There is also a slope to contend with. Mick would like to see it levelled, but this is not feasible as too much seating capacity would be lost. It is also part of the character of the ground and the one feature all visiting players remark on. There are two cranes still visible, two years on and Mick was amused to receive the following telephone call from Australia: "No wonder your ***** country is in such ***** trouble, you still have those two cranes there. You can never finish anything!"

Mick derives a great deal of pleasure from observing people looking at his handiwork, though he is still nervous before a big match. Batsmen and bowlers all want the pitch to suit them. So poor Mick receives plenty of flak and ribbing from them. The umpires have a system of marking the pitches on Test and One Day International matches. So far, Mick's pride and joy has always been marked 'good' and 'very good'. Before a match at Headingley or Trent Bridge, he always gives his opposite numbers a ring to wish them luck. Luck is always needed, but the care and devotion these men put into their pitches does not rely on luck but on skill, knowledge and sheer painstaking work over the months before a ball is struck and after a match, before another comes along to wreak even more havoc. No-one sets out to under-prepare a pitch. The Groundsman at Lord's, especially, is held in high esteem and with a twinkle in his eye, Mick, who loves curry, declares that he gets extra special service because they all know he works at Lord's.

If there is one place which is heaven on earth, in Mick's book it is, surely, Lord's at six o'clock on a summer's morning. And he is always there to see it.

LIFE'S A PITCH
The Groundsman's Lament

In Wintertime, in Wintertime,
The pitch is safe, the ground is mine,
No rude intruders spoil the calm,
The grass can rest, away from harm.

Come Spring, when nature is awake,
There are decisions I must make,
For hallowed turf to look its best,
Be in its prime before the Test.

The Summer's here and panic blind
With no more time to rest, unwind,
The ground prepared a brilliant green,
And now the public grace the scene.

The stage is set, too late for doubt,
I can't believe Lord Brocket's out
Am I to blame, is it too wet?
*Those b***** sprinklers, I'm upset.*

The game is over, Ashes won,
It was, they said, the greatest fun
I'm waiting round to take the flak
Quite undeterred, I will be back!

Anon

THE ADMINISTRATORS

Stephanie Ann Lawrence

The first impression of Stephanie Lawrence is of a woman who is completely and quietly, in charge, both of herself and her surroundings. She is slim, neat and correctly, though not extravagantly, dressed, in the manner of the well-heeled countrywoman. Her blouse is white and crisp, her jacket beautifully tailored and her jewellery discreet. This lady has a ready smile and a naturally authoritative air about her which must be a distinct advantage when it comes to doing her job.

She is Personal Assistant to the Secretary/Chief Executive of MCC and has fulfilled this role since 1967. When she first started at Lord's, she did PR for Jack Bailey, the Assistant Secretary under S. C. Griffith and at the same time worked for S. C. Griffith arranging major match hospitality for MCC, who also ran the England team. In other words, there was more than enough work to do. When Jack Bailey became Secretary, Stephanie was his PA. The Secretary of MCC was, in addition, Secretary of the ICC (formerly, the International Cricket Conference, now Council), which was entirely run and paid for by MCC in those days.

In 1976, Stephanie decided that it might be time for a change and duly went to the Brewers' Society in Portman Square, where she handled their publicity. She could not, however, completely cut her ties with Lord's, keeping up with her friends there. Jack Bailey also used to come to lunch at the Brewers' Society from time to time. The new job, Stephanie admits, was very nice but very boring.

What made Stephanie choose Lord's in the first place? Apparently, it was all the fault of a boyfriend. She was working, as a legal secretary, in Birmingham, the town to which she had moved aged five, from Sheffield where she was born on 7th March, 1946. As an only child, she had been shy and always ailing, until at the age of 13, she had her tonsils out and from then on, never looked back. She was educated at a convent, which she adored, though not a Roman Catholic herself. This convent, (Convent of the Holy Child, Jesus) was founded, of all things, by a divorced American. Stephanie joined in all the religious services and still loves incense and Latin but has not been influenced to be particularly observant. All her friends were gravitating towards London and her boyfriend at the time suggested that she might like to work at Lord's so that he could get free tickets to matches! She knew nothing about cricket as the nuns had not initiated their charges into the delights of the game, but nevertheless, went for an interview. This turned out to be non-existent and she was given a cup of tea and told to go home. They must have liked her, though, and been sufficiently impressed to take her on.

After her sojourn at Portman Square, she returned to work for Jack Bailey and continued on where she had left off. "It was not very original of me", she admits, "but I loved it". In 1987, nine years after her return to the fold, Jack Bailey retired early and Lt. Col. J. R. Stephenson took over. That year, Colin Cowdrey was President. The following year, it was decided that the ICC should have more of a role to play and Stephanie was taken on as Administrator, in charge of the day to day running of the organisation. This carried on until the ICC became completely independent in 1992. She moved back to being the Secretary's PA and to organising hospitality. Many other tasks, such as the MCC diary and Annual Reports, Stephanie did single-handed. There are now separate departments for the jobs she used to do. Stephanie's office is inside the extension to the Lord's pavilion, overlooking the main ground. It has a fabulous view, which helps enormously when one just wants to stop and stare for a minute or two. People ring her for everything, no matter how trivial, like names and addresses at Christmas time. There is, nowadays, no longer a PA job, as such. Whereas all letters were handed to the PA to be dealt with, the new staff now write their own on their computers. It has been said that Stephanie has a pivotal role in the running of Lord's by dint of the fact that she has been there for so long. She certainly knows all the wrinkles and the politics

and can steer a wise and diplomatic course through the demands of the job.

Stephanie is decisive in the work field, she says, but not in private life. She is loyal, honest and straightforward, though not overly tactful and she tends to see things as black or white. The bit about not being tactful may not be altogether true. As part of the hospitality job, when she sees single ladies in boxes, she puts herself out for them as she, personally, does not like doing things alone. She is very adroit at manipulating people, in the nicest possible way, a trait she has practised from childhood, according to her mother. When off-duty, she lives with her mother in Bidford–on-Avon, Warwickshire, ('drunken' Bidford, the Bard called it) and is a keen gardener. Her mother is immensely proud of her and even at her age, never stops rushing about finding things to do. When at home, Stephanie loves cooking for the two of them, and also for friends. She can spend hours dithering about what gastronomic delight to produce. One of her greatest pleasures is spending a leisurely evening with friends, with the ebb and flow of discussion and the food and wine all combining to produce the relaxed, convivial atmosphere she loves.

Stephanie has to retire next year, at 60 and it will be difficult for her to give it all up, but she plans to travel and be free to please herself, for a change. Maybe she'll opt for a bit of fly-fishing or bowling. She is a great friend of Sir Ron Brierley and goes to stay with him in Sydney from time to time. She has travelled extensively in the course of her work with the ICC to New Zealand, Australia, Sharjah and Holland for the ICC Trophy. It was the greatest fun travelling with Colin Cowdrey as he was always kept supplied with plenty of booze, but she seems to remember he never had a bottle-opener. Lord's is, obviously, her favourite cricket ground, but she is also fond of Worcester and Basin Reserve, Wellington, New Zealand.

"Lord's", she enthuses, "is a magic place. It is its own world and a wonderful institution. It is a huge leveller and so long as you like cricket, you are accepted at Lord's. It is a beautiful place, like an oasis. It is constant, but evolves and upholds high standards. It is one of the only great institutions left. The crowds accept the constraints and behave well because they know that Lord's is special and different."

Stephanie Lawrence is also special and will be a hard act to follow, indeed, an impossible act to follow because what she does not know about the inner workings of this great institution can be written on the back of the proverbial postage stamp. Those that come after her can always look up the information they seek, but they will not be able to go by the shortest route and do what everyone has always done – ask Stephanie

The Reverend Michael David Vockins OBE

ike Vockins is that dying breed, a Sporting Vicar. This splendid man, with thirty years of devoted service to Worcestershire CCC behind him, was drawn to the spiritual life while sitting at the back of the church where Eileen, his wife, played the organ every Sunday. She had been playing since she was 14 and 50 years on still does. They moved to a village near Worcester where the active family service was run by families themselves, instead of a Minister. Mike felt curiously drawn to that, and wanted to learn more. He was advised to 'go away and read'. Training part-time for the Ministry, he was ordained in 1988, while Secretary of Worcester. It seemed appropriate that he should develop his ministry through sport. Peter May, David Shepherd and Colin Cowdrey were all Christians in Sport, an organisation started by Andrew Wingfield-Digby, who inevitably earned the nickname of Wingers-Diggers. His job was to provide pastoral care to the cricketers and anyone else connected with them. 'Beefy', who came to Worcester after Somerset, was always asking him to 'say one for him'. Although not exactly a believer, Ian would do anything he was asked to do. He was always the first one to have a drink with the sponsors, if required and he often went out of his way to be kind. On one occasion, a terminally ill child, a lad of seven, who was not expected to live much longer, requested to come and see his hero, Ian Botham play. Ian talked to him, but the boy was so overawed that he remained speechless. He was taken to the dressing room, where Ian introduced him to all the players and gave him his bat. On another occasion, Eric Clapton, Elton John and the Electric Light Orchestra came to see 'Beefy' play. There were three Ferraris in the car park, that day, Mike remembers. After the game they went back to Ian's rented house, stuck out in the wilds (so that he could fish). Eric had left his guitar behind, so he bought one from a local shop (imagine the shopkeeper's amazement when Eric walked in). They all went down to the local pub and Eric played for everyone there – something the locals will never forget.

Mike, after leaving Oxford Polytechnic and working for five years, went to the University College of Wales, Aberystwyth, where he read agricultural biochemistry. At the end of the first term in 1966, he married Eileen and they have two daughters Helen and Morag, both married. Mike had played cricket ever since he could stand up and his father was a keen club cricketer, who encouraged both him and his younger brother. He played at school and at Highclere – in the shadow of the castle – where the village were allowed to play. This was an idyllic cricket ground and he has wonderful memories of that time and of playing good class club cricket around the Hampshire clubs. In 1970, he and two cricketing friends devised Six-a-Side Indoor Cricket and he was given the task of promoting it nationally. Lord's were snooty about it, but were convinced in the end. It has now found its way round the world, and Mike could never believe that something so simple and effective had not been thought of before. Mike also took an MCC coaching qualification, through Hampshire CA, run by Arthur Holt and Leo Harrison.

At Worcester, he captained the Club and Ground XI, which was a good way of getting to know young members of the playing staff and those who had come for a trial.

Mike has also toured abroad, as Tour Manager, with English Counties to Zimbabwe in 1985, a side captained by Mark Nicholas, spending a revealing morning with Robert Mugabe, having at an earlier time met the charismatic Ian Smith. Australia in 1990 with the England under-19s and New Zealand in 1992 followed the African trip. The England A team went to Australia in 1993, with a side which included Jack Russell, who became a good friend. On to Pakistan with Nasser Hussein, a wonderful tour Mike says, and one he would like to repeat. In 1996, he was awarded an OBE for services to cricket.

When Mike first went to New Road, his brief was to try and improve the club's PR with the public and local Press. He did manage to build this up strongly. On match days, he always walked once or twice round the ground so that he was accessible to the general public. Worcester did have its fair share of eccentrics – one Loppylugs, Archibald John Morrison, chartered accountant, Master of Hounds, and sometime writer for the *Horse & Hound*. He carried a hunting horn and whenever anyone scored a 4 or a 6, or a wicket fell, he blew it. He would strip off his shirt, put his braces on to his bare chest and run round the ground, 'to get ready for the beagling season!' Mike had to deal with some irate comments about this unusual man, but he never forgot that Loppylugs was utterly devoted to his paralysed wife and a stalwart of the Bromsgrove Boys Brigade. The hunting horn is now buried in the rose garden at Lord's after it was trampled on when he forgot which side he was blowing for and a fight between supporters ensued.

On arriving at his new job for the first time, he had a secretary/bookkeeper and one telephone and that was all. Everyone knew everyone's business and it was his role to guide the committee in terms of making policy. When he retired, there were 12/13 on the administrative side, physiotherapists, ground staff and catering staff.

"What a great privilege it has been", enthuses Mike. He has met so many wonderful people during the course of his cricketing and administrative time and alongside that has been the church role since his ordination. He now looks after three villages as Hon. Curate and Rural Dean of Ledbury and part-time college chaplain of Hereford Sixth Form College. In addition to all this, he has wanted to write and broadcast and is doing some of that, presenting a mixed bag of subjects from Jack Russell to agricultural chaplains who did such sterling work during the foot and mouth crisis in Herefordshire, which was particularly badly hit. He has done a programme on Edward Elgar the Countryman, of special interest to him as he and Eileen live in what was Elgar's summer retreat, where the great composer completed *The Dream of Gerontius*. As for holidays, if there are any, he tends to go walking somewhere in this country. He is passionate about Scotland and regrets that he was not born a bit further north, so that he could have been Scottish by birth. He had to make do with Cumberland and Berkshire, but he admits that he has had a lovely, lucky life and would not want to change a thing.

Michael Vockins with his sympathetic attitude, his capacity for listening and his fund of amusing and touching stories, has been an outstanding servant of Worcester, bringing in much-needed change and providing a sure and steady hand at the helm. His standards have always been of the very highest and he has sought to run Worcester as a club, rather than a business. Not that he is unmindful of the need for constant finance; it is more about creating the atmosphere of an old-fashioned cricket club, with all mod cons and everything of the best, but with the personal service of a bygone era. The telephone is answered personally and there is always a recognisable face to greet one at the desk. Players mix with the members after play, in the bar, not if they feel like it, but as a requirement. It is something they are expected to do and is one of the perks of belonging to Worcester so far as the members are concerned. Worcester is the most beautiful of all the country grounds and is often compared to the Adelaide Oval. This impression is enhanced by the fact that the grounds are so well maintained and painted each year. Flowers bloom in abundance and no member is left in any doubt that this club is exceedingly well run. They can thank the sporting vicar for that.

Terry Davies

The commercial and membership manager of the Adelaide Oval has come a long way; all the way from St. Albans in England via Glamorgan in Wales, in fact. Terry Davies, who used to keep wicket for Glamorgan, but could equally well have played football for West Ham, Spurs or Watford (if he had been larger, that is), decided to leave behind the country of his birth and settle in Australia, becoming a citizen. A Pom would have difficulty detecting any sort of accent other than Australian, but certain players have let it be known they think he talks cockney!

Born in St Albans, Hertfordshire on 25th October, 1960 his father came originally from Llanelli but moved after the war. He was an athletic Rugby Union player and he and his younger son spent a lot of time together, especially when it became clear that sport was going to be Terry's strongest suit. Terry was only nine years old when he announced to his uncle that he was going to become a professional cricketer. No-one took him seriously but Terry set about developing his natural talent for both soccer and cricket. Mr. Cooper, the games teacher, had a great influence on Terry and made sure that he met the captain of St. Albans cricket club, where he eventually became captain himself, opening the batting and keeping wicket. He was drawn to wicketkeeping because of the gloves. He loved them and loved wearing his mother's mittens too, when he practised for hours, throwing the ball at the wall in the back yard. Their neighbour was driven nearly mad with the continual 'thump, thump' of the ball. When Terry eventually turned professional, he always saw to it that his neighbour had tickets to all his matches. This was a typical Terry gesture.

After leaving school, armed with 'O' Levels, Mr. Cooper, who knew Len Muncer, ex-Glamorgan player who was Head Coach at MCC, recommended he have a look at Terry. He had a trial at Finchley, met Geoff Holmes, with whom he was later to play at Glamorgan, and they both found themselves accepted on to the groundstaff at Lord's. Jack Richards, a brilliant wicketkeeper at the time, took a great interest in him, but it was Kevin Lyons who took him under his wing at Glamorgan, where he coached the second eleven. He had been undecided as to which way to jump – cricket or soccer – and had toured Germany playing football, but was not quite good enough. He opted for Glamorgan, but was still not sure he wanted to be a professional sportsman. As there was such a lot of travelling involved, he had to think seriously about whether he could cope with this sort of life, or not. He could and he did. He was capped against the Australians in 1986 and played 100 first-class three day matches in all. In his first match, he put on 169 with 'Cads', Simon Daniels, with whom he shared digs in Cardiff. His greatest moment in cricket came when he was picked to play at Lord's. Javed Miandad, captain, told him he was in the side as wicket keeper. It was an incredible feeling to be playing at Lord's, to be a part of the long line of great players who have played there and to be on the players' balcony.

In 1986, he finished playing county cricket. The year before, wanting to escape the stereotype of his background, he took the decision to stay in Australia for good. Terry went to University at Woollagong and on leaving, landed a marvellous job as a sales rep. for Pacific Dunlop, progressing to looking after major accounts followed by specific projects. The company realised that he had a flair for brand and team building, and he ended up in senior management, living in Melbourne. 1987/88 saw him playing cricket for Bankstown cricket club, against the legendary Mark Taylor. The club could boast many famous players, including Steve Waugh, among their number. The club team contained nine first-class players. Bankstown became a successful club and earned respect locally by learning how to win. Terry now became, in 1989/90, State Selector for New South Wales. At a Sheffield Shield final, about to be played at SCG, the selectors had to decide who to drop and the choice came down to Peter Taylor or Greg Matthews. Terry had the casting vote and plumped for Greg, who was a proven match winner. He was at the SCG as a selector, when a message came over the PA system from the General Manager at Pacific Dunlop, that there had been a bomb threat because Peter Taylor was not chosen! However, his choice was vindicated when Matthews won the match for NSW. In 1991/92, Terry finished playing for Bankstown. His last match featured the greatest Bankstown team of all time against Australia. Between 8,000 and 9,000 people turned up to watch, among others, the Waugh twins and Jeff Thomson.

Terry met his future wife, Noelle, in England where she had come for a visit. His brother and sister-in-law lived in Sydney and Noelle and his sister-in-law worked together. Knowing that she was coming to England, Terry was asked to meet her at the airport and look after her, as she did not know anybody. Terry was playing for Glamorgan at the time and did his best to see that she came to no harm! It was his turn to go to Australia, where he was to coach for six months, and while there he looked her up in Sydney, and the rest, as they say, is history. They were married in 1984 and now have three wonderful children, Rhys, Rachel and Melissa.

SACA (South Australian Cricket Association) had advertised nationally for a commercial manager to be based at the Adelaide Oval. A consultant interviewed him in Adelaide, followed by all the Board members, and finally, he was offered the job. Terry was conscious of the fact that the job carried a lot of prestige, but, unfortunately, a cut in salary. He was willing to take this, he hoped temporary, reduction in salary because of the opportunity it gave him to be at the very heart of the game he loved, to be in one of the most beautiful cities in Australia, where he, Noelle and the children could settle down to a good life. Noelle supported all the moves and gave him help and encouragement along the way. She, herself, never really wanted a career, but she is a shrewd accountant and has more than enough work. Terry is now in his tenth year at SACA and still enjoying it. He does have ambitions, though, and is not quite ready to resign himself to doing the same thing for ever.

What makes this man such a good manager? He is bright and always interested in what he is doing and the people he meets as a result of his job. He runs the Adelaide Oval superbly, is always full of new ideas, has increased the membership to the point where there is a long waiting list and never, ever lets the grass grow under his feet. He is funny, lively, always willing to help out and, above all, loyal to his friends. For a while, he was Darren Lehmann's manager, until the job brought him into a conflict of interest situation, but they parted more than amicably and are still the best of friends today. He has a great personality, is one of the lads but the ladies rate him too.

If one wanted to draw a cartoon of Terry, it would show a small, alert, neatly-dressed man, a mobile to his ear and a bubble coming out of his mouth saying: "Hi, Terry Davies, SACA, what can I do for you? O.K. Sorted!" He is a fixer, a sorter-out of problems and, in his view, there is nothing that cannot be 'sorted'. Australia has given the Welshman from St. Albans a whole new take on life. There is no past, only the present and the future and Terry, still

ambitious, still relatively young, can probably, even now, achieve whatever he sets out to do. He is a huge asset to any firm and it is cricket's good fortune to have him safely tucked up in Adelaide, where he has made such a good life for himself and his family.

He has recently ventured into the art world and was the motivating force behind Jocelyn Galsworthy's 'Lords of Cricket' Exhibition. He introduced her to several Australian cricketers, whose portraits she drew to much acclaim and has been on hand with help and advice all along the line. She is immensely grateful to him for all his input. The word, 'sorted' has been music to her ears on countless occasions. In a speech at the House of Lords on the occasion of her Exhibition, Terry announced that some of the proceeds of the sale of her work would go to the Les Favell Foundation, in Adelaide, which supports disadvantaged children aspiring to play cricket and helps them develop their talent. Terry's own son, Rhys, is a promising cricketer and he feels strongly that other children should have the same opportunity to fulfil their dreams, too. With his feet firmly on the ground and his sights set high, he is an interesting man for whom nothing is impossible in life. His strength of character and his love for his family have taken him to where he is today and his unwavering optimism for the future will, with their help, see his ambitions fulfilled.

Terry Davies
b. 25th October, 1960 St Albans, Hertfordshire. England
Right hand bat
Wicket keeper

Lord MacLaurin of Knebworth DL

In his autobiography, *Tiger by the Tail* Ian MacLaurin states that ... "the future won't be denied. And never more so than in sport." When he was appointed Chairman of the UK Sports Council, in 1995, he found that it was a bureaucratic shambles, powerless to effect changes. A Labour Government was returned in 1997, and Ian, as a Conservative, thought he stood little chance of keeping his job. He decided to jump before he was pushed, but the whole episode with the UK Sports Council rankled with him, as he felt he could have made a difference if only people were willing to accept change. As a member of several MCC Committees, he knew only too well how conservative an organisation MCC was. Opening his mouth loud enough to be heard for once, during a meeting, he was slapped down by none other than Field Marshall, the Lord Bramall: "MacLaurin, this is a cricket club, not bloody shops."

Long ago and far away, Ian had wanted, for a brief moment, to be a cricketer. His father used to bowl to him in the garden, gently coaching and encouraging him. At his prep school he captained the cricket and the soccer sides. Again at Malvern, he found himself playing in the soccer and cricket teams along with boys three and four years older. He admits to not being 'academic', but this was more than compensated for by being so good at games. Those who could play games well were admired and respected by the whole school. The culture of deifying the sports hero was part of public school tradition and, to a lesser extent, remains so even today. George Chesterton and Dennis Saunders, cricket and soccer Blues respectively, had an enormous influence on him, he states. Chesterton came up to him in the pavilion one day and asked what he thought a good score for a batsman might be. Not wanting to sound immodest, Ian replied that he reckoned twenty-five or thirty would be a decent score. What followed was a revelation to the fourteen year old. He was told to think in terms of scoring a hundred when he went to the wicket, and not be content with second best. 'Always play to the best of your abilities'. These words of George Chesterton's have become the code by which he lives – never to settle for second best. Being naturally competitive, with an inbuilt desire to come out on top, might not be the best recipe for being a team player, he thought. But Ian was to discover where his real talent lay. He was able to lead from the front and motivate people, whether a cricket or soccer team, or a team of people selling something, without submerging his own, very strong, identity. Team building turned out to be one of the great strengths he brought to the job with Tesco.

In the summer of 1996, Ian was telephoned and asked if he would like to have his name put forward as Chairman of the ECB. This was to be a new appointment as it was, hitherto, known as the TCCB – Test and County Cricket Board. As he was leaving Tesco and keen to retire, he wasn't sure. More people rang and, eventually, he was persuaded to let his name go forward, but only if all the county chairmen agreed with his agenda. He had lunch or dinner with them all, one by one and as the result was satisfactory, his name went onto the voting paper and he was duly elected Chairman. Tim Lamb was already on board as Chief Executive. However, even if the TCCB had transformed itself into the ECB, the mindset was still the same. When, in 1997, Ian expressed a desire to join the England Tour to Zimbabwe, and what is more, wanted to stay in the same hotel as the players, he was met with silence. This improper suggestion had completely thrown them. It was explained to him that, "the management always stays in a different hotel". The reason for this became only too clear when he finally got there. The hotel chosen for the players in Harare was basic, to put it mildly. Two players were expected to share a very small room, with intermittently-functioning air conditioning, when the ambient temperature rose to 110 degrees Fahrenheit on occasions. Ian thought he would discuss the accommodation and also the game plan with the captain, Mike Atherton. Atherton confessed that Ian was the first person to ever talk to him about either subject. Ian was shocked at the treatment the players had to endure off the field and also the lack of leadership which, in his opinion, made a significant contribution to the poor performance of the England side in the Test series. The media, too, seemed intent on stirring up as much trouble as possible when certain players' behaviour occasionally let the side down. When they couldn't find anything to say, they made it up as they went along.

Ian, quite rightly, saw his next task as raising the profile of the England Team and in this he carried the Chief Executive with him. There seemed to be no pride in their sweater or cap, any more. They wore any old helmet to bat and it was not good enough. A strict dress code was henceforth implemented. They were to wear the England cap, helmet or sunhat and all wear the same colours in order to brand the England team and make sponsorship easier. True to form, Jack Russell had something to say about losing his trademark white hat, but this was resolved in the end to everyone's satisfaction. David Graveney as Chairman of Selectors was charged with the duty of informing players of any decision affecting them, before the press got hold of it, which was not always the case in the past, by any means. Any new cap a player earned was to be presented to him before the start of the Test match, instead of merely leaving him to help himself from a box dumped in the dressing room. Where was the pride in that? Team spirit was what counted. Ian knew this and set about fostering it and who better to do so than a man with a proven track record in team building.

Two-thirds of the way through the summer of 1997, Mike Atherton told the Chairman of Selectors that he wanted to resign as England captain. He had had enough. Zimbabwe had been a fiasco, and England's defeat by Australia at Trent Bridge was the last straw and Atherton the camel with the broken back. Ian tried one last time to persuade the stubborn Lancastrian to change his mind. He did and won the game at the Oval, in three days. Now, if he wanted to, he could leave on his own terms.

The summer of 1997 also saw the publication of *Raising the Standard* – a development plan for the game which would, ultimately, hopefully, result in England becoming the most successful and respected cricketing country in the world. The plan took in, as a starting point, schools, clubs and upward to counties and, finally, Test level. It is an encouraging fact that more than a million and a half youngsters play cricket (400,000 of them girls) and it is vital to keep the encouragement going along with the support they need to see their enthusiasm grow. From these beginnings come the future Test players, so it is important to have the groundwork in place. Ninety-five per cent of these proposals were accepted, but the counties rejected five percent and it was this small percentage which was fastened on by the dreaded media and the rest of it was forgotten.

Without their income from the ECB, the majority of the counties would have gone under long ago. For the last thirty years or so, they have been talking about reform, now here was a plan to achieve just that and they were rejecting it. The eighteen first-class counties were so jealous of their independence, they would not let the ECB determine anything to do with their domestic playing arrangements or their finance. The favoured option was the two-division county championship, but this was rejected by the counties in favour of an all-play-all county championship, with the top eight playing in a Super Cup in 1999. This formula resolved nothing, according to Ian, and it was back to the drawing board. Sponsors were beginning to lose interest and there was a real danger that, unless something was done, the first-class game would suffer terminal decline. This made negotiating the best deal for the TV contract for coverage of the game, particularly important. It was due to be renewed in 1998, but being on the government's A-list, restricted coverage to terrestrial channels, whereas the B-list was open to anyone. The BBC had been covering cricket for years and feelings ran deep. Chris Smith, Secretary of State responsible for Sport, was concerned that those who could only afford terrestrial television might lose out if contracts went elsewhere and those people had to be taken into consideration.

Nevertheless, he took the decision to switch Test cricket to the B-list. Channel Four produced much the most attractive bid and six out of seven Tests would be shown on terrestrial television, thus satisfying Chris Smith. However, in 2005, the ECB have plumped for an exclusive deal with BSkyB, because of the sums involved.

What about *Raising the Standard*? If things continued as they were, the first-class game would be in serious trouble. Falling membership, too few spectators and an image problem would see to that. At a meeting of The First-Class Forum, measures were adopted to transform the first-class game: measures such as an increase in the number of home Tests and one-day internationals and contracts for the England players with the ECB. All that remained was for the county chairmen to vote for a two-division county championship. They did, with only two abstentions Ian breathed a sigh of relief now that they were on the right track, but he knew they could never be complacent.

The criticism of not being a 'cricketer' in the widest sense has often been levelled at Ian. He not only understands the game through and through, but played in his youth for the Kent second X1. As the first 'genuine' businessman to become involved in English cricket at the highest level, Ian had to fight the sort of entrenched ideas which had, in his opinion, held cricket back and prevented England from being at the top of the Test cricketing nations. He introduced contracts, which meant that Test players were not worn out by non-stop games for their counties; he established the Academy at Loughborough, money for which was raised through Sport England; he 'branded' England so that the players had a real sense of identity and he was responsible for the change in the way players are treated on tour. He also appointed Duncan Fletcher, the highly successful England coach. That there was more to be done, Ian had no doubt. It was a great pity that he was not going to be at the helm much longer. It must be extremely galling for Ian to hear, in 2005, that Sport England have warned the ECB that they risk losing government funding, if they do not loosen the grip of the eighteen first-class counties on English cricket and its budget. *Plus ça change....*

In 2000, he became Chairman of Vodafone, which must have taken up a great deal more of his time than he had thought, and in 2002, he did not stand for re-election. Always having to consult and gain the approval of the counties for every decision, was a frustration to him. He was succeeded by David Morgan, a former chairman of Glamorgan and deputy Chairman of the ECB.

As well as his passion for cricket, Ian is also a mean golfer, but not as good as his wife, Paula, he says. He loves the Opera and goes whenever he can, as well as patronising the theatre in Bath. He is also very fond of his horses, which he used to race under National Hunt rules, but he now prefers to breed and has a couple of nice foals to be going on with. He and Paula are great supporters of a charity called 'Hope for Tomorrow', run by a family friend, Christine Mills. After a devastating personal loss, she wanted to help people cope with cancer when it is first diagnosed. This can be a very lonely time and literature and DVD's with all sorts of helpful advice are now placed in oncology units in the Gloucestershire area. Lord and Lady MacLaurin are the Chairman and Patron, respectively. Through The Vodafone Foundation, they are involved in Save the Children, whose Patron is the Princess Royal. 'I Can' is another charity helping children with learning problems, with which Paula has been involved for many years.

Ian MacLaurin is an outstanding man and an exceptional human being. He appears to have endless patience with people, going out of his way at times to help and support them. He never seems to be in a hurry, which is surprising, considering all he has to do, but it is part of this man's charm that he has time to listen. He would acknowledge that he has come a very long way. From a trainee to Chairman of Tesco, one of the world's most successful supermarket chains, now Chairman of Vodafone, picking up a knighthood and a life peerage along the way. He must have a core of steel and an extraordinary amount of drive and ambition to have achieved so much in the field of business. His time spent as Chairman of the ECB saw radical changes being introduced, with the good of the players as well as the prestige of the country in mind. Ian is certainly not a controversial figure so far as the players are concerned. He said of himself that he was no academic. Would he have been so ready to face life's challenges if he were? Sometimes, being too cerebral can hinder one's progress in the real world. Nothing, it seems can hinder Ian's progress, not even the fact that he is now 68. He still looks young, fit and vital and certainly not ready to doze on the back benches of the House of Lords, just yet. After all, Ian said it himself, "There is no future in standing still!

Lord MacLaurin of Knebworth
b. 30th March, 1937, Blackheath, Kent
Right hand bat
Left arm slow

THE MAGNIFICENT MEDIA

Peter Alastair St. John Baxter

Peter Baxter was born on 8th January 1947 in Derby. His father was a colonel in the Army and the whole family was just home from serving in Palestine. They were soon off again, to Austria for two years and then on to Cyprus. He went to Summerhill Court Prep. School at Haywards Heath and on to Wellington in 1960. By the time he left, he had already applied to the BBC on the strength of a talk he had heard at school, given by an Old Wellingtonian to two or three people who were vaguely interested in a career in broadcasting. It had been assumed that Peter would follow in his father's footsteps and go into the Army, but his father was dissuaded from any such idea, mainly to spare the Army. The family were now stationed in Aden, and Peter joined the Forces broadcasting station for three or four months, having a marvellous time. Within a week, at the age of 18, he was producing a morning record show and had to write the script for the announcer. It was a very good introduction to the career he wanted to pursue. The BBC asked if he could type, he couldn't but replied that he could, anyway. On being asked to prove it, he managed, very slowly, with the aid of two fingers and informed them that he had gone for accuracy rather than speed! He told them that he would like to do news or outside broadcasts. They put him into the outside broadcasting unit in radio, as a clerk. The programme department worked closely with the engineering side in those days (1965), servicing other departments doing outside broadcasting.

He used to be sent out to do all manner of jobs, not all connected with sport. It could be news, or looking after Margaret Thatcher on Budget Day. As Opposition Minister for Education, she explained to everyone what the budget meant and Peter found he had enormous respect for her intellect. Eventually, he landed the job of Assistant Producer in the same department and worked on the weddings of Princess Anne, Prince Charles and Prince Andrew. He also did funerals. Working on a quiz show 'Treble Chance' and its offshoot, 'Forces Chance', he went on a tour of the Far East – Gan, the Maldives and Singapore. On his return, he was asked to go to Test Matches in the place of the cricket producer, Michael Tuke-Hastings, who hated the game. Test Match Special had started in 1957 on the third network and by switching wavelengths they were able to get every ball. Beginning in 1973, Peter was asked to join the team, at the age of 26. Johnners probably had a hand in his appointment so that he got someone compatible. By this time, Johnners was a very old hand and it was a bold choice. Peter has been doing the job ever since. Everything that goes into putting a programme on air is Peter's responsibility, such as briefing and picking commentators and engineers. His job, though, is not always recognised as being important. On one occasion, arriving at Lord's, one of the car park attendants asked if he was a commentator. When Peter said he was the producer he heard the reply "Oh, just a producer. I suppose you come along to watch." Far from it, he is responsible for all the cricket coverage going out on BBC network radio. This can mean anything from running a radio network when TMS is on the air to briefing architects on the construction of a new commentary box to emptying ashtrays and producing cups of coffee. On a TMS day, he is handed the long wave frequency of Radio 4 from 10.55 a.m. until the end of the day's play, apart from the News and the Shipping Forecast. If rain stops play early, they can rejoin the normal FM programmes, but rain breaks and intervals must be filled in and this is where initiative plays a part and Brian Johnston came into his own with all the amusing business with cakes and 'leg overs', Holding and Willey. Blowers too, pontificating for ages one wet afternoon failed to notice that everyone had left the box and became panic-stricken when a note was shoved in front of him which read; "KEEP GOING TILL SIX O'CLOCK". Peter sometimes felt that he had a necessary, additional role as schoolmaster in the Lower Fourth.

While relaxed banter is going on in the TMS box, elsewhere, in another commentary box, his team has to provide reports for Radio 1, Radio 5 Live and the BBC World Service (and some of its foreign language services) as well as regional and local radio programmes. They can't put their feet up in the winter, either. There is commentary on all England's overseas Test Matches, however difficult that may be to achieve – self-wired ancient equipment in Guyana, or a telephone in a corridor in Lahore or even a ledge in a clock-tower – a feat of which Peter is enormously proud.

Peter has two children, Claire in her last year at Birmingham, who wants to go into journalism and Jamie, a useful cricketer, who is on a gap year before going to Leeds University. Peter likes gardening and generally doing things about the house when he has a break from working. He loves rugby and was a rugby producer for eight years, also producing the Boat Race for ten. At the moment, the retirement age is 60 and when that comes round, Peter would like to do some writing, inevitably about cricket, or match reports for a newspaper. His favourite cricket ground is first of all, Lord's, closely followed by the Adelaide Oval. He loves the beauty of Worcester, but says it is difficult from the broadcasting point of view and that detracts from its charm.

Peter feels immensely privileged to have known and worked with John Arlott and Brian Johnston as well as some of the overseas commentators like Alan McGilvray (his mouth crammed with cake just as Johnners asked him a question) and Tony Cozier. What other job could he have done, given that his job, in his eyes, is undoubtedly the best.

Henry Calthorpe Blofeld OBE

The last of the old-fashioned, faintly errant Test Match Special stalwarts, Henry Blofeld ('Blowers') is as distinctive as John Arlott or Brian Johnston. Brought up in the era of Gentlemen and Players, this endearing character has, nevertheless, adapted to modern times rather well. Summarisers and statisticians notwithstanding, the Test Match Special commentary box when he is there carries on the marvellously descriptive traditions of the late John Arlott who was a poet, author and wine connoisseur, but above all a cricket broadcaster. 'Blowers' has a voice and accent redolent of a different era and all the better for it. He has a global following, which may surprise the sort of people who are impatient to modernise everything, including the style of commentary. Brash and Blowers are opposite ends of the spectrum. There is something so comforting about being able to listen to this extremely knowledgeable man, particularly if you are of the same vintage and know that England and cricket have not yet changed out of all recognition.

'Blowers' was born on 23rd September, 1939, the day that petrol rationing was introduced. War had been declared but had not yet been felt in Hoveton St John, Norfolk. He felt that he had been a mistake, his older sister beating him to it by ten years and his brother by seven. He grew up in a wonderful world of what would nowadays be called privilege – on a large estate with wildlife to observe and in season to shoot, the Broads, the farm and the characters such as Carter, the gamekeeper who used to bowl to him and was umpire at village matches on Saturdays. The indoor staff at Hoveton, the cook, the parlourmaid and, most importantly, Nanny, coloured his early life. He was always slightly frightened of his father, but when he died, his mother assured him that his father had been 'very fond of him'. He was, in fact, a most courteous and interesting man with a fondness for PG. Wodehouse, which he used to read to Henry before bedtime.

Henry was introduced to cricket during his first term at Sunningdale, the prep school in Berkshire, a goodly proportion of whose boys ended up at Eton. He made the first XI and gained much respect and also had a turn at wicketkeeping which was a revelation to him. Next stop Eton, where his brother John had left such a good academic record that Henry felt he could never live up to what was expected of him. He spent two years in Lower Sixpenny and was made captain, graduating to Upper Sixpenny with another captaincy and on to Upper Club and the first XI. At 15 he was asked by the captain whether he would play in the forthcoming Eton-Harrow match at Lord's. For Henry, then, life could simply not have got better.

Returning to Eton for his last half in the spring of 1957, he was captain of the first XI and had made a century at Lord's (Southern Schools v The Rest) when the unthinkable happened. Cycling to net practice before playing Marlborough the following Saturday, Henry collided with a bus full of women from the French Women's Institute and that was the last thing he knew before he woke up in the King Edward VII Hospital in Windsor. He had been severely injured. His mother and father were looking round Chartres cathedral at exactly the time the accident occurred. In fact, his mother, who had never done such a thing before, was lighting a candle. Typically and unsentimentally, Henry refers to the whole thing as being 'very French!' He recovered well and King's Cambridge had, mercifully, decided to forgo the entrance exam because of the accident. That was a relief. Henry went on to play for Cambridge, acquiring a cricket Blue and scoring a century against MCC at Lord's. He also played for Norfolk.

On leaving Cambridge, Henry decided to try working for a firm of stockbrokers in the City and received a tip from his mother about a company in the Far East, originating from her local hairdresser in Norfolk who got it from a client. He decided to invest a little money in this rubber company himself. The tip proved correct and his personal stock with his employers rose markedly. Henry managed to play cricket, get married, have a fairytale time in Jamaica (his hostess having chucked out Richard Burton and Elizabeth Taylor to make room for the newly-weds), meet Noel Coward and Ian Fleming, whose character Ernst Stavro Blofeld was named after Henry's father. Hopefully, the similarity ended there. Investments and banking had now lost their appeal and Henry, bored out of his mind, thought it might be time to try his hand at something else. He flirted with the wine trade but calculated he would drink all the profits and himself into an early grave and realised that, actually, all he had ever been good at was cricket. Why not write about the game for a newspaper? Easier said than done, but, happily, a meeting with Johnny Woodcock who kindly offered to help was to turn out to be a godsend. After proving to himself and *The Times* that

he could write a satisfactory account of the cricket match between Kent and Somerset at Gravesend in 450 words, relay it to the copytaker not more than forty-five minutes after the end of play by telephone, he was up and running. He has written, variously, for just about every national newspaper, joining Test Match Special in 1972 and has been there ever since apart from a break when he was on Sky. He appears on television from time to time, on such shows as 'Countdown' where he sits in Dictionary Corner and 'Ready Steady Cook'. His many books all sell well and *Cricket and All That* reached the Top Ten Bestseller List. He was Wine Correspondent for the *Oldie* Magazine – a subject he knows as intimately as cricket – and is a humorous and witty after-dinner speaker as well as having his own One-Man Show, 'An Evening with Blowers' which plays to packed houses.

This endearing and highly civilised man, who always seems to sport a bow tie and call his friends 'my dear old thing', has been an inspired addition to the TMS team. Far from being the relic of a bygone era, he has more energy and drive, despite his recent heart trouble, than many men half his age. But his brand of energy does not include shoving and pushing to achieve his goals. The man, who might have played for England at the highest level, does not envy others or curse the cruelty of life. He gets on with the job he loves and which he does so well. It is significant that, when he returned from his stint on Sky Television, there was a collective sigh of relief as he was heard once more describing the buses, the pigeons and anything else that took his fancy. Occasionally, this ran to women and once, commentating alongside Sunil Gavaskar, probably in India, he was about to burst forth with a remark which would pass unnoticed in England but would be scandalous further East. On seeing a good-looking woman, he started his verbal run-up, realised his mistake but it was too late – he had to go on. He did the only thing a gentleman could do. 'What an enchanting pair... of earrings'. Sunil could hardly contain himself.

He married Bitten, who is Swedish, in October, 1990. His daughter Sukie is from his first marriage and by all accounts a marvellous cook. He is a loving stepfather to Bitten's son, Alexei, known as Rumple and, for all that he seems forever 'on the go', he loves being at home at Hoveton, where he now runs the shoot. He particularly hates being away at Christmas. In 2003, he was awarded an OBE for his services to broadcasting, a deserving tribute for a man who is almost as much of a broadcasting institution as the chocolate cake in the commentary box.

Henry Calthorpe Blofeld
b. 23rd September 1939, Hoveton St. John, Norfolk
Right Hand Opening Bat

Christopher Dennis Alexander Martin-Jenkins

Christopher Martin-Jenkins has written about cricket for over thirty years and is acclaimed both as a Test Match Special commentator and as a cricket journalist, writing as Chief Cricket Correspondent for *The Times* and contributing articles to the *Wisden Cricketer* magazine. He was born in Peterborough on 20th January 1945. His father was Chairman of Ellerman Lines (Shipping) and his mother a doctor, from a long line of Peterborough doctors. His father was a keen cricketer who played club and village cricket and the young Christopher was passionately keen on the game from an early age. He was educated at Marlborough, captaining the First XI and making an unfortunate score of 99 at Lords against Rugby. He read history at Fitzwilliam College, Cambridge, played for the Cambridge University Crusaders, but sadly failed to get a Blue. Playing in the Surrey second XI was fun but he realised that he was, to all intents, only an amateur. Once he started work, cricket was precluded. However, he does have the satisfaction of knowing that his son Robin plays for Sussex, having gone to Radley and Durham University just before Andrew Strauss.

Christopher began by being Deputy Editor of *The Cricketer* (later to become *The Wisden Cricketer)* from 1967 to 1970, a BBC Sports broadcaster for the next three years and two stints at being BBC Cricket Correspondent from '73-'80 and again from '84-91. A spell at *The Cricketer International* followed, first as Editor and then as Editorial Director. From 1991-1999 Christopher was Cricket Correspondent for the *Daily Telegraph* until he had an offer from *The Times* he couldn't refuse. There was also some friction at *The Telegraph* arising from the constant editing of his articles. Christopher is lucky to have gone all round the world in his capacity as commentator and journalist, though not while the children were small. Memorably, he recalls the Ashes being won while he was on air (at least twice, if not three times). In the TMS box, he is one of a team consisting of Henry Blofeld ('Blowers'), Jonathan Agnew and Peter Baxter the producer, as well as Bill Frindall, the statistician, and Vic Marks the summariser. There will also be someone from the opposing team's country – when it was the West Indies recently, the commentator was Viv Richards.

Christopher has written twelve books to date: *Sketches of a Season* was illustrated by the former England and Gloucestershire wicket-keeper, Jack Russell. *Summers will Never be the Same* was edited jointly with Pat Gibson and was an affectionate and amusing tribute to Brian Johnston in the form of contributions from those in the world of cricket who knew him well. Peter Baxter wrote that 'he became, at once, the moving force behind Test Match Special – the catalyst for almost everything that happened in the box. Brian would sit down at the microphone and take events as he found them. He may have seemed to be the great amateur, but in so many ways he was the most professional of them all, always the first to arrive and prepare for the day's play ahead. There were gentle and subtle chidings for any colleague who in Brian's view went a bit too far. Christopher Martin-Jenkins described the apogee of a ball's flight and must have regretted it over the next ten minutes as the mutterings went on behind him. "Apogee. What a good word. I wonder what he's talking about." Every day was fun to BJ. It will be the best tribute to his memory if the tremendous generosity of his spirit can be preserved in the Test Match Special commentaries.'

That Christopher is an acclaimed after-dinner speaker is well-known, but what may not be such common knowledge is that he is an excellent mimic. This may stem from his days at Cambridge as a member of the Cambridge Footlights, along with Germaine Greer, Clive James and Eric Idle of Monty Python fame. His thespian activities may well have contributed to the ease with which he handles life in front of the microphone. His commentaries are very good and well worth listening to.

Christopher belongs to several clubs, MCC, I Zingari, Free Foresters, Arabs, Marlborough Blues, Cranleigh Cricket, Albury Cricket, Rudgwick Cricket, Horsham Cricket and West Sussex Golf. He is President of the Cricket Society and a Trustee of the Arundel Castle Cricket Foundation. He must find it extremely hard work keeping up with them all on top of his broadcasting and journalism duties. He is very much a family man and lists as one of his relaxations, 'the family', along with music and the open air. What will he do when he retires? There are no mutterings about this possibility yet; however, once a writer always a writer and so more books are more than likely on the cards. Perhaps he would like to try his hand at a novel, set in the cricket world, of course. Meantime, he will continue

to educate and elucidate on air during the cricket season. Perhaps he will be at the other end of the microphone when the little urn, locked away safely at Lord's, is claimed. Ah, but by whom?

Christopher Dennis Alexander Martin-Jenkins
b. 20th January, 1945, Peterborough
Right hand bat
Right arm medium/offspinner

Jonathan Philip Agnew

If you thought that Jonathan 'Aggers' Agnew was merely a voice on Test Match Special, then think again. He played first-class cricket for Leicestershire between 1978 and 1990 and represented England in three Tests between 1984 and 1985. He was the most consistent English pace bowler in county cricket in '87 and '88, but he was ignored by the England selectors, despite needing fast bowlers. In 1984, he won his first caps against the West Indies and Sri Lanka and the following summer made his final appearance against Australia. Why did he give up cricket? It was a sad fact of life that he could not manage on the salary he was being paid and when he asked for a raise, it was refused.

'Aggers' did a stint on local radio, Radio Leicester, at the invitation of John Rawling, BBC commentator, athletics and boxing, for a while and thoroughly enjoyed the experience. He was able to play for Leicester and the following winter, 1987 presented a sports programme which went out from 2-6pm. His book *Eight Days a Week*, written in 1988 was a highly acclaimed, entertaining take on the life of a County Pro. 'Aggers' was the first cricketer to go abroad as full-time correspondent for *Today*, a now defunct tabloid. They were pleasant to work for so he thought he would take a chance on going to Australia with them in 1990-91. When Christopher Martin-Jenkins left the BBC to join the *Telegraph*, Jonathan applied for his job to become BBC Cricket Correspondent. It is a particularly interesting job as it appeals to different audiences and the programme is varied according to whether you are on Radio 4, Radio 1 or Radio 5 Live.

Very often Jonathan is required to go to places where there is trouble like Zimbabwe. He wrote a piece *From our own Correspondent*, usually the preserve of the intrepid Kate Adie, which he loved doing. He spent a week holed up in a hotel in Cape Town following the Zimbabwe cricket and political scenes and had to be wary when it came to unscripted comments as it is so easy to 'put your foot in it.' In January, 2003 he was at the microphone in Sydney, just as Steve Waugh was trying to make his century, which he achieved with the very last ball of the day. Jonathan thought him an amazing cricketer, whom the Selectors were trying to dump. He was so gritty and determined and put so much pride into wearing the baggy green. Kerry O'Keefe, former Australian leg-spinner, was summarising and though usually talkative, was silent at this moment of truth, charged with emotion. But Waugh triumphed and was picked for the next Tour. The feedback to the radio station was fantastic – people stopped their cars to listen to a great sporting moment.

Jonathan was born in Macclesfield where his father was a dairy farmer and the best sort of sporting father you could wish for, joining in without pushing or overdoing things. Jonathan's enthusiasm for cricket originally stemmed form his father. When he was 12, his father took him to watch a Gillette Cup Final. Peter Lever of Lancashire became his absolute hero, to be copied at all costs. Later on 'Aggers' met Peter Lever, who he said was the nicest of men. 'Aggers' played village cricket, (men's cricket) when he was 14 and at 16 he was taken to Alf Gover's Indoor Cricket School at Wandsworth. Alf got on to Surrey who signed him up for their second team at £20 a week, during the school holidays. He was signed up to play County Cricket when the coach at Uppingham, Maurice Hallam, who played for Leicestershire, told the captain about this new young fast bowler.

His job at the BBC suits him down to the ground although, having said that, much of the excitement, spontaneity and spirit of adventure has disappeared. Everything is much more regimented and 'professional', but the shorter Tours do have their advantages for a journalist. He has met dozens of people who have impressed him from all walks of life. Sport on 4 did a piece "Sport on Robben Island" where Jonathan met the first black Minister of Sport and Mayor of Cape Town as well as Nelson Mandela. He found them to be very impressive and keen on the idea that sport, above all things, was a unifier of peoples, regardless of colour. Wherever in the world England go to play, Jonathan goes too, but in personal terms he thinks this might have led to the breakdown of his marriage. Now his employers are far more understanding of the problems created by being absent abroad for so long and his new wife, Emma always comes with him for two or three weeks. Sometimes a broadcaster's life can be fraught with danger – he was required to play in goal when he did a feature on a men's hockey team. This put the wind up him but he managed and even enjoyed it after a while. Test Match Special is highly enjoyable, and Jonathan typifies the 'endearingly juvenile approach' of the TMS team, seeing the funny side of everything. This is hardly surprising when you have the master of schoolboy humour and amusing aside, the evergreen late, great Brian Johnston to live up to.

One thing Jonathan does not approve of is the 'dumbing down' of cricket. Cricket is the ultimate challenge for the individual playing in a team sport – a trial of his skill, bravery and mental strength. Cricket exposes your character and weaknesses like no other team sport and, as such, its standards must be kept up. There is no need, in his opinion, for raucous music every time someone scores. It is a thinking game, played on beautiful grounds, why ruin it by blaring out utterly meaningless pop music? Test Match Special and the BBC try to remind people of the tradition behind this wonderful game and the ECB should follow suit. It is not about appealing to the lowest common denominator. Jonathan very much hopes to continue in broadcasting, which is his niche and at which he is so very good. People listen in from every conceivable place, even Antarctica. Submariners call in regularly and pilots listen to him in their cockpits. When he gets an email, though, he wishes he could be like Brian Johnston and think of an instant, witty reply. He could always say, "Never bowl your Granny a full toss, even on her birthday..."

Jonathan Philip Agnew
b. 4th April, 1960, Macclesfield, Cheshire, England
Right hand bat
Right arm fast
Commentator
Wisden Cricketer of the Year, 1988

Dr. William Howard Frindall MBE

Bill Frindall insists that he was named after a dog. His parents had been expecting a girl and had chosen the name Susan Florence Elizabeth, but they got a son instead and were stumped. Now, he is known as 'Bearders' or 'The Bearded Wonder' because he has one and is one with his cricket statistics which are second to none.

It all began at Primary school. His Headmaster played club cricket for Epsom and coached the boys, but one rainy day when cricket was impossible, he detached some pages from a note book, drew out a score sheet and invited the boys to learn how to score. Most of his companions were bored but not Bill. While his parents went shopping, an aunt took him to a club to watch cricket. "Can you score?" he was asked. "Yes", replied Bill, "I learnt to score last Tuesday". He must have done rather well because they kept him on and gave him ginger beer at the end of the match. In the fullness of time, Bill won a scholarship to the Kingston College of Art, but he only wanted to design cathedrals. When he took a job with the Lutterworth Press, he had only been there five weeks and the production manager disappeared. Happily, or perhaps not, he was conscripted into the RAF to do his National Service and they offered him a choice of Dental Officer, Clerk Accounts or Clerk Progress if he signed on for a further year. Which would give him the best opportunity to play cricket, he asked himself and chose Clerk Progress. Bill says he was 'Horlicks' on the parade ground, walking with a bounce and nervously getting his hands in the wrong order. However, he went to RAF Benson in Oxfordshire where he had a good time, playing cricket for Abingdon Town. On to Northolt where he opened the bowling and was eventually sent to France. His team beat the British Army of the Rhine who were the Cup holders and also Holland, before lunch! He was, by now, Flying Officer Frindall, or as Bill put it, F.Off. He was the accountant officer for RAF Leeming, editing the *Leeming Lights* magazine. He also checked the Chaplain's inventory and found that he had, somehow, lost an organ and gained an axe... The camp magazine was rated so highly it was even mentioned in the national press. When the RAF offered to renew his commission, he felt it might be time to leave as his father had just died and, in any case, he really wanted to concentrate on cricket.

Bill was given an interview by the Head of Outside Broadcasting at the BBC and told that they would like him to cover County matches for which he would be paid eight guineas a day. Brian Johnston was present and asked impossible questions, forcing Bill to redesign his bowling sheet, when he insisted on knowing how many boundaries each bowler had conceded. At the time he was working for Legal and General, for whom he had also kept score and played. He was a Life Insurance Inspector – making sure the agents were conjuring up business – and playing cricket in the afternoons. He kept records of the MCC team touring in Australia and his records did not agree with the official statistics. He visited the official compiler's office and it was a shambles. Bill then rang the editors of *The Times*, *Guardian*, *Telegraph* and *Express* and they all agreed to pay for his services. His figures were compiled on the train going to work and by noon were neatly typed (he took the typist out to lunch, occasionally). He soon learnt that he had cornered the market as no-one else was doing these statistics. The *Daily Express* then asked Bill to write for them

In 1966, Bill met John Arlott for the first time and knew they would get along famously. Arlott enabled him to buy a complete set of scores and biographies for £28, treating him as a surrogate son. For his last appearance, a Taverner's match, he was airfreighted over from Alderney where he lived, his fee being a case of red, and after four bottles, fell asleep during his commentary. One of the comments Bill will always remember John Arlott by is the perfect cartoonist dismissal – "drew him forward, crossed him off and rubbed him out."

Before the great Brian Johnston, there used to be canned music in the commentary box instead of banter and a fund of stories as the rain came down. This coming season will be Bill's 40th, making him the oldest member of the Test Match Special team. He provides statistical information for those engaged in doing the commentaries, but also gets the chance to put in a word every now and then himself. He is called 'The Bearded Wonder', or 'Bearders' as Brian Johnston would have it. He has his own way of scoring which he has copyrighted and also edits '*Playfair Annual*'. He has been introduced, on occasions, as the Editor of 'Foreplay Annual.' He had four years setting the questions to a radio show, 'Sporting Chance' for schools. Bill is also the Cricket Archivist of the Paul Getty estate at Wormsley.

He met his wife Deborah, 'Debbers', in 1978 and they have a daughter, Alice aged 9. His main wish is to live to see his daughter grown up. He would also like his autobiography, due out in 2006, to be a roaring success. With Bill Frindall's

fund of funny stories, innuendo and double entendre, coupled with a life well lived, there is no doubt of that.

Bill is lively and interesting but you never quite know whether it is Harry Secombe or 'Bearders' to whom you are talking. The eyebrows shoot up as does the voice in a Neddy Seagoon falsetto and if you are not careful, you will hear a raspberry and get your bottom pinched! As long as

this does not happen in the Test Match Special Commentary box, then he is forgiven.

Dr. William Howard Frindall
b. 3rd March, 1939 Epsom, Surrey
Right hand bat
Right arm medium fast

Edward Patrick Eagar

When Patrick Eagar's cricketing father, Desmond, was called up during the war, his mother lived with her parents just outside Cheltenham. His grandmother recorded in her diary that "Marjorie walked to the Imperial Nursing Home from Charlton Kings" (quite a step), where he was, subsequently, born on 9th March, 1944. After the war, his father had a choice between playing for Worcester and Hampshire, having played for Gloucestershire before. He chose Hampshire, where he was captain from 1946-1957. During his lifetime, he amassed an amazing collection of cricket books, which are due to be auctioned by Christie's. Some of the books are so rare that not even the British Library has copies, among them a score book published in 1799, recording the details of cricket's earliest matches.

Patrick, having been brought up on a cricket ground and a member since 1946 of Hampshire, would watch matches all the time. When he visited Hampshire in 1986, he decided to take a few photographs, but was soon challenged by a grumpy member demanding to know what he thought he was doing.

Patrick enjoyed his little prep-school at Swanage, then graduated to Cheltenham College, which was not quite so much fun. He did well enough to get a place at Magdalene, Cambridge reading Natural Sciences, taking time out to photograph anything that moved – cricket, rugger, rowing, athletics, theatre and girls. On leaving Cambridge, he went to work for an agency called 'Report', which sent him off to Vietnam in 1966. He went with a British Medical Team and did four months' worth of features for the *Illustrated London News* of 1966, and for anyone who wanted photos. James Cameron had been sent to North Vietnam the year before and had interviewed Hoh Chi Min. The agency was founded by Simon Guttmann, originally from Berlin, but who had fled in 1943 to England. He was not very 'commercial' and neither is Patrick, so they got along well. While he was working for Simon, he managed to do some cricket photography of his own, largely as a result of Jim Swanton. This

generous man was keen to see young people get on, either in journalism or, as in Patrick's case, photography. He did work for *The Cricketer*, thanks to Swanton and when *Wisden Cricket Monthly* started, he was asked to come on to the editorial board, where he still is, although the magazine is now known as *The Wisden Cricketer*.

It was next to impossible to get near Lord's, The Oval or any Test Matches to take photographs because of an agreement between Lord's and The Oval which carved things up between them, excluding outsiders. This arrangement came to an end in 1972. When Patrick and others were, finally, let in, they had to turn up to every match as part of the deal. It was a small price to pay and, in any case, Patrick felt he already had a head start as he had been photographing cricket for many years. From then onwards, he has had luck on his side, he maintains. The modern camera has revolutionised the sporting photograph and colour film has done the rest. Before Patrick came on the scene, photos tended to be taken from an elevated position, but he always took them from ground level. In the early days, there would be, perhaps 8 representatives of the various newspapers at a Test match, but now it is more like 30 or 40.

Going to Australia in the winter had been an option for Patrick, but he did not take it up. In 1972/73, he went to the West Indies (who were playing Australia), for two Tests, and as the West Indies were coming to England in 1973, Patrick reckoned he could, perhaps, sell features. It was expensive to travel then, but once there, the colour and atmosphere seduced him and it was great fun to photograph and something people had not seen before. He got to know the players but their managers and the press were something of a pain, as they tried stop people poaching on their preserve. His next trip came in 1974/5 to Australia this time, as a freelance photographer for the *Sunday Times*. He had done two summers' cricket for them and he told the editor, Harry Evans, that he was going to Australia and would send them photos. The Editor begged to differ, but Patrick got his way in the end. The first Test was at Perth and he sent back very nice pictures of Doug Walters making a fast hundred. The pictures were very tiny when they appeared, as the *Sunday Times* did not think they would arrive and had not left enough space! When his pictures from Melbourne landed on the Editor's desk, they had reserved eight columns. In those days, cricket photography was at the unfashionable end of the spectrum. Everyone wanted to photograph Jean Shrimpton and be David Bailey, so Patrick was very much on his own, breaking new ground all the time. Post Offices ran a picture transmission service, unchanged since the thirties. It was quite quick, taking about eight minutes, but Patrick had to stand over people and make them do it. This was

the forerunner of today's digital transmissions. It only really worked on black and white. Sending colour photos was difficult and nowadays it is ridiculously easy.

Photographic equipment was improving all the time, better lenses and cameras, and it was important to keep abreast of all the innovations. Since one never really knows what will happen next in cricket, Patrick had devised a ploy of leaving his camera in a certain part of the ground, which could be activated by remote control. The first time he did this, at Maidstone, it needed 300 feet of wire, but now one can use a radio connection. They are unreliable, though, and can go off by themselves and take all the photos in five minutes, using up all one's very expensive film. In Adelaide, sad to say, he had his camera stolen. During a centenary Test match, against Australia, he decided to take a group photo of 200 people, players and others, at Lord's. The idea had come to him on seeing a similar photo in Australia and he discussed the concept with Sir Donald Bradman. Col. Stephenson was most helpful and the project took off. Unfortunately, some of the players were late, or had forgotten about the sitting but most of them turned up. He wanted to take one photo in black and white and one in colour, which was such a slow process that the cricketers were bored out of their minds. In the end, four large copies were made: two are at Lord's, one in Melbourne and one in Sydney.

Patrick has kept everything he has ever taken, carefully filed and indexed, which can be sent anywhere in the world at a moment's notice. Some people have never heard of copyright and used to use his photos without permission. He says he could pay his airfares out of lost revenue from pictures published in magazines without his knowledge.

He has two children, Kate a graphic designer and William in animation and editing. He plays golf off a 14 handicap and has a great interest in wine and vineyards. This was encouraged by none other than that great wine buff, John Arlott, many years ago. He has been to all the great wine-producing areas, Australia, South Africa, Chile and Argentina, France and last but not least, Sussex, photographing vineyards and viticulture, selling his pictures to books, magazines and newspapers. He thought it would be fun to have a vineyard of his own, but is not keen to rush into retirement just yet. Having said that, since everything is such 'big business' today, he feels lucky to have started when he did, in an era of no competition to speak of, when he could shape his own future as he liked. This genius of the lens has been a steadfast servant to the pictorial representation of the game and justly deserves the title of greatest cricket photographer of his time.

Mark Charles Jefford Nicholas

Mark Nicholas is a very busy man – having been a successful and very popular captain of Hampshire, writing for the *Daily Telegraph* while still playing, he now writes features for the same newspaper, talks about cricket and commentates for Channel 4, hosts television programmes such as 'Survivor' and has recently joined Australia's Channel 9. This is a great honour as Mark is the first Englishman to whom such an invitation has been extended, when England are not playing.

Mark was born on 29th September 1957 to a mother who was an actress. His father died when he was only eleven and this had a traumatic effect on him. He was educated at Bradfield and acknowledges a debt to his housemaster there, Chris Saunders, who was a real friend to him, buoying him up and keeping him going when life got tough. His stepfather, too, Brian Widlake, who hosted 'The Money Programme' was a great mentor, guide and support. As a child as young as seven, Mark discovered that he had a talent for impersonating the cricket commentators. He found that he understood the game even then and had made up his mind that he would, one day, play for England. On leaving school, Mark knew that all he wanted to do was to play cricket and, as his mother did not want him to go to university, his housemaster who had played cricket at Oxford and knew the Hampshire captain, arranged for him to have a trial. He had to bowl at Barry Richards and was so nervous that he could not let go of the ball. He batted very badly too. Nevertheless, he was put in at number 5 against the Kent second eleven at Dover. He made a hundred as did Chris Cowdrey, playing for the opposition. With his sporting background in the shape of his brilliant grandfather, who as an all-rounder played football and competed in the Olympic Games in the long jump and sprint, and his mother's talent on the stage, the scene was set for Mark to shine in both spheres. This he has done to an impressive extent. He was a very talented cricketer at county level, achieving 36 first class centuries, one first class 200 and 1,000 runs in a season, ten times. In 1985/86 Mark captained the England 'B' tour to Sri Lanka and the England 'A' tour to Zimbabwe and Kenya in 1989/90. Although he had many offers to captain other counties, he remained loyal to Hampshire. He never did get to play for England at the highest level, despite the ambitious target he gave himself as a boy.

The second part of his career began with Sky television. Mark is a highly professional performer. His clean-cut good looks and his sartorial style –he once kept his smart, flannel blazer on in temperatures reaching 46 degrees – go a long way to making him particularly popular with the female audience and those who may not know very much about the game. He explains the intricacies carefully and even arranges demonstrations to avoid any ambiguity. He recently persuaded the hapless Muralitharan to demonstrate his style of bowling (which has caused so much adverse publicity) to the viewing audience by encasing his bowling arm in a plaster cast, or something very similar, and asking him to bowl his trademark 'doosra'. Mark could see nothing wrong with his action and even had a bowl himself, wearing the cast. Mark once said "I think I bowl, but no-one else does!" However, *quod erat demonstrandum* and the case for the defence was well and truly made.

His entry into the world of Sky nicely illustrates the determination with which Mark seems to approach everything. It is possible that if one has a thick skin it helps, but it is more likely when one is in the right place at the right time. He went to see John Gayleard, the producer of cricket for BSkyB to see if he would give him a job. No luck, no vacancies. Mark plagued John Gayleard daily to no avail until suddenly, because someone was ill, he found that he had a day's work at the Test in Adelaide. Mark found himself in the middle of a daunting array of famous names: Bob Willis, Ian Chappell, Allan Border and David Gower. He got through it in such style that he was asked to do the next day, then the next Test and, eventually, the whole series. He stayed on after the cricket was over to cover the tennis, Gayleard offered him a permanent job at 2 o'clock in the morning. But Mark was contracted to play for Hampshire. Gayleard was contemptuous of that. "Get out of it", he snapped. Mark was with Sky Sports for three years until he had an offer he could not refuse from Channel 4. The big attraction there was that he had a blank sheet, *carte blanche* and was able to be involved in the editing and the final cut as it appears on screen. He is proud of what he was able to do and proud of the way he has been able to make the programmes more accessible to those who do not, necessarily, understand the game. He is now working, during the winter, for Channel 9 in Australia.

As with all walks of life, every time it appears that someone is having more than their fair share of success, sniping and jealousy are never far behind. Mark is accused of being arrogant, whereas he would say that he is merely

self-confident. Men, in particular, are always making fun of his hair. This is, clearly, a case of jealousy of the worst kind. The Nicholas genes have endowed him with abundant locks which show no signs of falling out, receding or getting threadbare. On one occasion, there was much merriment in the Test Match Special commentary box, when the pitch became unacceptably damp. The groundsman started drying it with a hand-held hair-dryer, for all the good that would do. One commentator turned to the other. "Where did that come from?" "Must belong to Mark Nicholas", was the reply.

Mark loves music. He will go anywhere to see Bruce Springsteen and has seen him perform live once or twice. He even managed to wangle a half-hour private chat after one of his shows. He goes to live concerts often, having led his team mates astray on one occasion when five of them and their captain went to see Michael Jackson in Cardiff after playing Worcester. They were stuck in a traffic jam coming out of the city at 11.30 at night, drove round the countryside looking for petrol, woke a slumbering petrol-station attendant up after he had gone to bed, and got back to Worcester at 4.00 in the morning. What a sight they presented, five chaps and their captain the worse for wear and beer! He has grown up since those days and now his preference is for wine and his fondness for 'Down Under' must mean that he has the opportunity to compare New World wines to his heart's content. The theatre, not unnaturally, is another love of his. He has never married, recognising that his lifestyle and the exigencies of his work would not make for contented domesticity. Or is it because he knows himself too well? He has expressed the desire to get behind the camera and to direct or produce. It might also be time for a book.

Mark Charles Jefford Nicholas
b. 29th September 1957, London, England
Right hand bat

THE SPORTING KNIGHT
&
THE PHILANTHROPIST

Sir Michael Ronald Stoute

ir Michael Stoute is something of an enigma. As a Bajan, a native of Barbados, that beautiful coral island set in the Caribbean, with white sand beaches, turquoise seas and a balmy, tropical climate, he could have remained in the country of his birth, immersed in the national sport, cricket, and lived an undemanding life, perhaps following in his father's footsteps. His father, Major Ronald Stoute, was Chief of Police and had his residence close to the racecourse at Garrison Savannah where racing was staged in the 1890s between the Regiment and the Plantocracy. The horses for the Mounted Police were kept on land belonging to the residence and they were the young Michael's first introduction to the animals which were to play such a huge part in his life. As young as six, he would also watch the racehorses exercise every morning and, in his words, "I was hooked". In his teens, Michael started race calling in Barbados and Trinidad, with some success and, when he finally decided to seek fame and fortune in England, he put himself forward for the job of BBC Television racing correspondent. He was required to call a National Hunt race at Newbury on a bitterly cold afternoon, and was totally out of his depth having never seen this particular form of racing before. He failed to get the job. Michael may have been upset at the time but his rejection by the BBC set him on another course which was to bring him amazing success and financial reward. He is, at the time of writing, champion trainer for the seventh time, has won twenty-four Classics and numbers among his owners The Queen, HH The Aga Khan, Prince Khalid Abdullah, The Weinstock family and the Maktoum family.

How did the Master of Freemason Lodge arrive at this happy destination? "Luck", he says. Like most great men, Sir Michael tends to hide his light very firmly under the proverbial bushel when talking about himself. He is genial, funny, animated and charming but never smug or self-satisfied. He has a kind of restless energy coupled with a certain laid-back way of talking still retaining a Bajan lilt to his speech, which is very likely much stronger when he is conversing with his countrymen. His great friend in the cricket world, Michael Holding, who is a keen racegoer, rents a house opposite every summer and it must be most amusing to listen to the Barbadian and the Jamaican discussing the merits of the West Indian team in their particular dialects. Sir Michael is softly spoken and one cannot imagine him losing his temper very often, certainly not with the horses. His owners get results from him, not flannel. He cannot abide having to tell owners that their horses are not performing and leaves all that to his Assistant Trainer. He tells a good story about Lord Weinstock who felt that he had not heard from his trainer for a long time. When Sir Michael telephoned and said who he was, Lord Weinstock replied, "Michael who?" There was a long pause, then he continued, "I once had a trainer called Michael Stoute, but I haven't heard from him for so long I thought he was dead!"

Sir Michael's other passion is cricket. Growing up in Barbados in the forties and fifties, he remembers that everyone played cricket during the lunch break at school and on the beach before swimming. It was while playing for Harrison College he developed his 'stylish' bowling technique. Equally, one could watch real cricket at the Test ground very easily and frequently, with a variety of matches on offer from Colts through to first class inter-island and Test matches. In England, a visit to a Test ground is a big occasion and only happens once or twice a year, whereas in Barbados the accessibility of the Kensington Oval meant that one could easily see the great players in the flesh and be inspired by them. His great hero was Everton Weekes, one of the three W's (Weekes, Worrell and Walcott), all born in the same year within a few miles' radius of one another on the island of Barbados. This fact has impressed Sir Michael deeply. There was real fervour for the game which is lacking to some extent today, although cricket is still the national sport and still very popular, particularly when visiting Test teams come to the Kensington Oval. The good news is that money will be allocated to completely upgrade this Test ground where the Final of the World Cup will be played in 2007.

Sir Michael plays for the Newmarket Trainers' X1, which he captains whenever time permits. Sadly, his bowling action seems to have been lost, he tells us, due to his mucking-out duties while learning his trade in the late 1960s! In 2003 he brought his celebrity team, including Rory Bremner and Michael Holding, to the Centenary Week of The Royal Household Cricket Club Frogmore, the

Queen's private ground at Windsor. Five matches featuring different teams were to be played over seven days, all for various charities, Sir Michael's being the Injured Jockeys Fund, of which The Queen is Patron. The Royal Household CC ground sported a new extension to the pavilion and a marquee where 200 people were seated to lunch and tea on each day. The main sponsor of this prestigious event was John Spurling of the Lord's Taverners, but many more individuals and companies donated handsomely to ensure the success of the week. Her Majesty came to lunch and tea on several occasions, including the Newmarket XI day and appeared completely relaxed while watching the cricket, something she rarely has time to do. She seemed to enjoy the informality and knew many people well. John Taylor, Chairman of the Royal Household CC, had been Page to the Queen since her coronation and, of course, Sir Michael as her Trainer would have helped on that score.

During another charity match playing for the Lord's Taverners, Sir Michael first met Rory Bremner. He is a great admirer of Rory's astute and wicked impersonations. On this occasion, fellow Taverner John Ketley, the weather man, was the butt of his caustic wit. In Barbados Rory was once interviewed during the tea interval and was extremely relaxed and hilariously funny. It is quite possible that the Bajan trainer himself is in line for being sent up, if Rory has not already succumbed to the temptation...

January is relaxation time for Sir Michael. The flat season has not yet started and England is at its most uninviting, weatherwise. He has just been to South Africa to watch cricket in the sunshine at Newlands in Cape Town, one of his favourite cricket grounds. Kensington Oval comes top of his list, followed closely by spectacular St. Vincent. St Lucia and even Nevis now get one-day internationals. He is all for encouraging the smaller islands to take their place on the cricket map. His love for the West Indies and their Test team is evident and he longs to see them great again, revitalised and ready to dominate in the way they did so successfully for some 20 years from the mid-70s.

Sir Michael has been a wonderful ambassador for his native island and has made such a significant contribution that he was knighted in 1998 by the Queen for his services to sport and to tourism. Would Sir Michael have wanted to be anything other than the highly successful racehorse trainer that he is? Well, if truth be known, he would have liked a career as a professional cricketer. That he was not quite good enough is cricket's loss and, undoubtedly, racing's gain.

Sir Michael Rnald Stoute
b. 22nd October 1945, Barbados
Right hand bat
Right arm slow, deliberate

Sir Ronald Alfred Brierley KT

We all have to start somewhere, and Sir Ron Brierley is no exception to this irritating rule. On leaving school, at 17, he landed a job in an insurance company in Wellington, New Zealand as an office boy. Instead of studying accountancy, he thought it would be better to acquire practical experience and started applying for jobs for which, he says, he was not qualified. He got an accountant's job, when he should not have, and pretty soon he knew that he wanted to go into business for himself. New Zealand in the forties and fifties was extremely conservative, with no frills to soften the rather severe environment. It was in the fifties that he discovered the stock markets when they were more individual, but he didn't think much beyond the New Zealand Exchange. Nowadays the markets are trading worldwide and all influencing each other. This is part of the worldwide communications revolution in which computers have played such a major part.

At 18, he started up a newsletter in stocks and shares. He felt that people would read the newsletter and if they liked the ideas they read about, they would invest in the company to implement these ideas. He wanted to be an active participant in order to create change. Things were very slow to begin with, very few investors and life was tough, but he thinks this was a good thing. It was a fantastic learning process for him, and a painful one at times, because the media delighted in targeting him and his ideas. Tough as this learning curve was, he did not give up. He had an essential philosophy about asset values in relation to share prices. Prices often undervalued the true worth of a company, which should be judged on performance, not on intrinsic value. He never wavered from this philosophy and, eventually, it came right. He says he would never have been content with being a stockbroker, which after all, is just an agent. The natural progression was to a company of his own. Brierley Investments Ltd. became a huge company which brought its own problems. It was a public company from the outset, but people were unwilling to invest. It was like mining gold – lots of dirt for a few, tiny nuggets. The 1960s were difficult years but the tide was changing by the 70s. What Sir Ron did, so effectively, was to acquire control of already substantial companies and then improve their commercial performance.

Sir Ron's father had played club cricket in a modest way and it was natural that he should gravitate towards the game. He lived in Wellington until he was 26 and says that he was, originally, going to be one of the greatest Test players that ever lived, but somehow, business got in the way. He had to content himself with cricket as a pastime, instead. He was roped into the fringes of New Zealand cricket, his commercial success making him able to assist them financially. One thing led to another, he got to know more and more people connected with the sport and he became a Trustee of Sydney Cricket Ground. He now lives permanently in Sydney, which he loves, and has a house on the harbour. He is Chairman of the Guinness Peat Group, technically a U.K. company, but the communications revolution means that you can be anywhere and still do the same things with the same people.

Sir Ron Brierley is one of the great benefactors of the world and considers it a great privilege and pleasure to be able to help. Arundel, to name but one club, says it does not know what it would do without him. He promises he will try to be more involved on a personal level with Arundel and will try to get there more often. Meantime, he insists that their cricket foundation ought to be supported to a larger extent by the England Cricket authorities. He still plays cricket occasionally, and he put in a playing appearance at the Royal Household Centenary Match for 'Swan' Richards (Robert Richards) side, The Crusaders, of which he is an honorary member. They play all round Europe, Ireland, Scotland and England, and bring two teams so that they can play two at once. The Crusaders are not to be sneezed at; they are a good side, playing at club level, with a smattering of ex-international and ex-first-class players among their ranks. The standard is pretty high. Swan asked the Prime Minister of Australia to write to the Queen about laying on a fixture at her private ground at Frogmore. Nothing was heard from the palace, so he went to see Her Majesty personally. A fixture was agreed, but on insisting that the Queen and Prince Philip attend, he was told that only a minor royal would be there, if anyone at all. Legend has it that the Duke of Gloucester's Secretary was advised by the Secretary to the Queen that his employer should not go. "Don't go, the Boss is doing it!" The Queen appeared for the first time in 1989 and has been to every fixture (every two years) since then, except one, when she had to go to Canada. She has been tremendous in her support and she says, reputedly, that it is one of the happiest weeks of her year.

Sir Ron still supports New Zealand cricket, despite living

in Australia and was President of New Zealand Cricket in 1995/6, the centenary year, which unfortunately, proved to be an absolute disaster.

He has no more grand plans or ambitions. He just wants to go on enjoying life in a trouble-free environment. Marriage has not entered the equation – his brother, who was in the Navy as a meteorologist, has children and a dog – that is quite enough to satisfy him so far as family goes. He likes the mental stimulation and intellectual challenge of chess and he would enjoy writing a factual book but not a novel, which would require a different set of talents. Curiously, he dislikes public speaking because he feels 'a bit of a phoney'. Conversely, he does not mind public meetings, as Chairman of a company because then he really does know what he is talking about. Although he has horses in Australia, he does not really have any great interest in racing. This must be the only thing Sir Ron does without his whole heart being in it. The impression he creates is of a very modest, private person, who, although sensitive to what is said about him in the media, will not go out of his way to read about himself. He claims never to have looked himself up on the internet, which must, surely, be unusual in a businessman with his finger on the pulse. Perhaps not, as Sir Ron Brierley is the kind of man who does not need anyone to tell him that he is a success. His efforts have seen his company grow into a multi-billion-dollar operation. As he quietly goes about his life, making a great many philanthropic gestures, this unassuming and rather understated man can rest in the knowledge that he is putting back a large amount of what he has taken out, and has a great many admirers on the strength of it. He can do this because, in his own words, with a shy smile, "I've done rather well".

Sir Ronald Alfred Brierley
b. 2nd August 1937, Wellington New Zealand

THE DOYEN

John Charles Woodcock OBE

John, Woodcock, who will be 80 next year, has lived his life in Longparish in a house which has been in his family and a village where his family have appointed the parsons since the middle of the 18th century. Even doing something as attractive as going off to write about cricket overseas – he covered forty tours for *The Times*, sixteen of them to Australia – came as a wrench, because it meant leaving Longparish. He has written for *The Times* for more than fifty years, and still gives them a number of pieces a year. "The time has gone horribly quickly" he says. "*The Times* have been very long-suffering. You had to be pretty bad for them to sack you in the old days," he says in his self-deprecating way.

His education was entirely Oxford-based – at the Dragon School, St Edward's and Trinity College, where he read History and Geography, "a sportsman's degree" that went out long ago. He went on to take a Diploma of Education, with a view to teaching, but changed tack and switched to the world of cricket writing when taking a job with Jim (E. W.). Swanton, as his "dogsbody". It was with Jim, to Australia in 1950-51, that John went on his first tour, doing some writing of his own as well as taking a BBC camera with him and flying home film of the Test matches for television news, the first time this had been done. On getting back to England he made a film of the tour, *Elusive Victory*, which was widely distributed around schools and clubs.

While at school himself he had picked up a virulent infection – "a vicious war time bug" – which entered the system through a blister worn while playing squash and turned rapidly into full-blown septicaemia and septic arthritis. It was well before the days of modern antibiotics, and for some time his life hung in the balance. The legacy was a steadily increasing arthritic condition which restricted his own cricket career, although he won a Blue for hockey at Oxford, keeping goal, played golf to a lowest handicap of 8 and played at most other games. He has also fished the Test and Wiltshire Avon with long and uninhibited enthusiasm. He gives his recreations in the reference books as "golf and country pursuits".

In time, new hips became necessary, the first in 1955, with others following in 1967, 1969, and 2004. He lays claim to two unique hat-tricks: the first to have been given new hips by three of the greatest of all orthopaedic surgeons, Sir Henry Osmond-Clarke, Sir John Charnley and Mr John Read, and the second to have played golf with Yorkshire's three greatest opening batsmen – Herbert Sutcliffe, Sir Leonard Hutton, and Geoffrey Boycott.

In 1952 John joined the staff of *The Manchester Guardian*, now simply *The Guardian*, as London Sports Editor, reporting the 1952 Test matches against India for them. This was made possible by the contacts he had made in Australia. Ten years later, he himself was to help Henry Blofeld into journalism, but not into broadcasting, which "Blowers" did through his own strength of personality. In April 1954 John joined *The Times* as their Cricket Correspondent when the Sports Editor died and the then Cricket Correspondent, Geoffrey Green, moved into his job, leaving a vacancy for John to fill. These were the days when the England team still travelled to overseas Test matches by boat, a much more leisurely and civilised way of doing things. One had time to acclimatise and get to know the players. Today, the whole cricket scene is far more pressurised and intense, but John does make a great effort to keep abreast and not to become, in his own words, "a dinosaur". The last time England sailed on tour was to Australia in 1962 on the *Canberra*, after which an era passed away, never to return.

John and Henry Blofeld had become great friends, so much so that in October 1976 they and three other brave and perhaps somewhat foolhardy friends decided to drive from London to Bombay to meet up with Tony Greig's England team at the start of their tour of India. Through a friend and neighbour of Johnny's (as Henry always calls him), they went in a claret and black 1921 Rolls Royce Silver Ghost, while their friends drove a new three and a half litre yellow Rover, known as "The Yellow Peril".

The route they chose wound its way through France, Austria, Yugoslavia and Greece to Istanbul and through Turkey, Iran, Afghanistan and the Khyber Pass into Pakistan to Lahore and Delhi through Rajasthan to Bombay. Such a journey today would be almost impossible when one thinks of the nature of the governments of at least two of the countries on route. Nevertheless, in 1977 where there was a will there was a way. Helped by a donation in kind from one of their sponsors, Long John Scotch Whisky, the path through Customs was sometimes miraculously smoothed, as were the ruffled feathers of the intrepid party. When, finally, they pulled up outside the Taj Mahal Hotel in Bombay they had covered 7,867 miles in 46 days, after which The Yellow Peril and Silver Ghost were shipped back to England while Johnny and Henry toured India with the England side.

Just before John returned from another tour of India, the Editor of *Wisden* died. Soon afterwards, at a reception in the Long Room at Lord's to celebrate the marriage of Brian Johnston's daughter, he found himself speaking to the man who would be appointing the next Editor. John was asked whether he would consider taking on the job himself. Although nothing of the kind had ever occurred to him, he would, and he did, editing the publication for six years from 1980. His assistant editor, Graeme Wright (who became Editor) was invaluable to him and he admits he could not have done it without him. He found himself doing his job at *The Times* as well as editing *Wisden*, and when this became too much he gave *Wisden* up.

John has never written a book, although he co-edited, with Jim Swanton, *The Barclays World of Cricket*, and a book was made by *The Times* of his hundred greatest cricketers and also of his reports on the Test matches against Australia in England in 1956. He has seen many changes down the years, television bringing one of the most influential. Previously, when writing about a tour, or anything else outside England for that matter, no one had actually seen the action. Now, with everything being so closely and widely monitored on television, journalists are expected to look for angles – or so he was told! It was not, he is ashamed to say, a forte of his. But he feels immensely privileged to have been on so many tours, to have witnessed so many great matches, met so many great men and made many marvellous friendships. His life has been full and rich. His one real regret is having no children. Being away so often on tour – usually for several months at a time – was no life for a married man. So far as his writing life goes, there are issues that he feels he should have reported differently and better – though one wonders about the second of those sentiments.

Henry Blofeld, in his amusing autobiography *A Thirst for Life*, attests to the fact that he has had more fun with Johnny than with anyone else he has known in all his years with cricket. A wonderful tribute to an old friend. Johnny Woodcock, that shrewd observer of the game and most excellent of cricket writers, is held in highest esteem by fellow journalists, cricketers and members of the public alike. But being the modest man he is, he would probably not think so.

THE ENCYCLOPAEDIA

Christopher David Evelyn Bazalgette

Known simply as 'Gette' from his cricketing days, Christopher Bazalgette is a marvel. At the age of 66 he still plays for the Hampshire Hogs and holds the record for wickets taken, probably 3,500. He cuts a distinctly old-fashioned figure (no trips to the gym or personal trainers for him), has old-fashioned manners and speech and is, at a guess, one of only a handful of people who know the game and the characters in and around it like the back of his hand. Ask Gette anything to do with cricket and he will give you the right answer – and a lot more information besides.

The name Bazalgette comes from a small commune, La Bazalgette, in the Massif Central of France although the family seat was further south at Ispagnac. In 723AD, one of his forbears was commander of the forces which kept the Moors, who were sweeping through Europe, at bay. His family crest shows a lion rampant with his paw on a crescent, depicting the crushing of these invaders from the east. In 1789, at the time of the French Revolution, two members of the family escaped to England and settled in Suffolk and Surrey. Another had already gone to America to seek his fortune, grew very rich, history does not furnish details, returning as a tailor and finding himself one of a growing number of outfitters who lent a great deal of money to the self-indulgent, extravagant and perennially impecunious Prince of Wales. Christopher's great, great grandfather followed in the Bazalgette tradition of derring-do and, as a naval officer, cut out a ship, *The Sphinx*, from the French fleet in the Mediterranean in 1814, while his grandfather (1819-1891) was a very famous engineer responsible for the eradication from the Thames of typhoid and cholera, both deadly waterborne diseases. He provided London with 5,000 miles of drainage and, in recognition of his great service to the nation, a bust of Sir Joseph Bazalgette now resides permanently on the Embankment.

Christopher, himself, was born on 24th November, 1938 in a nursing home overlooking Edgbaston cricket ground; an auspicious beginning for someone for whom cricket has been the passion of his life. He lived in Solihull and was educated in Southampton and Thomas Hardye's in Dorchester. After leaving school, he went into the Army with a view to making it a permanent career (as his father had done) and joined the Household Cavalry. Halfway through his training, after playing three games of rugby in three days, he found that one of his legs refused to bend. He was encased in plaster, the normal treatment in those days, but eventually, this damaged his kneecap. Five operations to the left kneecap later, he was invalided out of the army with a 50% disability pension. This notwithstanding, he had a further ten years of the sport and finally gave up rugby at the age of 35.

His first job was teaching cricket at a Prep school, where the captain of Yorkshire's son was one of the pupils. When he left, he went in a completely different direction, opening up a branch of Securicor in Birmingham. He resigned after only a year. In 1972, he started his long association with *The Cricketer* magazine. He worked for *The Cricketer* for 32 years without a contract, merely a handshake with the managing director and chairman of Brock, the parent company of *Sporting Magazines*. He was advertisement manager, also writing articles on major topics such as coaching, cricket equipment and clothing. These themes were expanded and developed to become Tours and Touring and Ground Equipment. The Gette genius for invention took off and Christopher set about redesigning the sight-screen (which had become prey to vandals at cricket grounds). His screen now sells all over the cricketing world. Not content with that, he has recently designed an aid to fielding for which he wrote his own patent. This device replicates a batsman facing a bowler. It is a triangle of wood, three or four feet high with bullnose corners. When the ball is bounced at one of the corners, it will glance off at an angle, making the fielders concentrate. Christopher says that his invention is essentially different from the existing slip cradle in current use. Unfortunately, it has not gone into production because Christopher has yet to find the right person to make it.

It is fair to say that Gette eats, sleeps and breathes cricket. Not that he does much sleeping. Rather, he catnaps and works all night. This must be somewhat disturbing for his wife, June, whom he married on June 19th, 1965, on which day there was a Test Match in progress. No-one could find Christopher and there were a few anxious moments, but all was well in the end. They have a daughter, Fiona who in turn has given them a granddaughter, Thea, a source of great joy to them both.

As one would expect, Gette belongs to many cricket clubs in England and around the world. He is an honorary member of Hambledon along with David Gower, and honorary member of The Willows, Richard Hadlee's cricket club in New Zealand, The Auckland Cricket Society in North Island and the Crusaders in Melbourne. Nearer

Christopher Bazalgette.

Jocelyn Galsworthy
2004

home, he is a member of MCC, Chairman of Cricket for the prestigious Forty Club and Chairman and founder of The Bat and Ball Cricket Club at Broadhalfpenny Down, in Hampshire, after the famous pub of the same name. Hambledon was where cricket changed from a pastime into a sport, when certain eighteenth century noblemen got together a side from within a forty mile radius of

Broadhalfpenny Down and called it Hambledon Cricket Club. The Bat and Ball Cricket Club was started in 1993 and in 1994 the area manager for Ind Coope, the brewers who owned the Bat and Ball pub, thought it would be a good marketing wheeze to change the name of this famous watering-hole to 'Natterjacks.' Since Broadhalfpenny Down had been the home of cricket long before Lord's, it was felt that this sacrilege could not go unpunished and middle England rose to a man in defence of their shrine to the Noble Game. Letters arrived from near and far, protesting at such a preposterous idea, Brian Johnston rang the Today programme in a fury and even the Almighty (surely a spin bowler) got in on the act. The whole area was flooded for six months and no-one could get in from the south. Sales plummeted and, finally, Ind Coope decided to sell the pub to another brewer, Geo. Gale & Sons, who were much more sympathetic. The Bat and Ball was safe and the storm subsided.

Christopher has had a lot of fun playing cricket over the years. It is amazing to watch how slowly, yet how devilishly he bowls. He describes himself as an away-swinger, an action which catches many an unwary batsman off guard. Christopher Martin-Jenkins, the well-known cricket writer, once wrote that he ran at the same pace as the Queen Mother, who was nearing 100 at the time... In 1979, he created and organised, together with Wynne Williams and Christopher and Roger Thompson, The International Batsman of the Year competition held at The Oval, for which Courage had put up £100,000 in sponsorship. The idea was that 8 leading batsmen had to bat for a certain number of overs and the one who emerged with the highest score was the winner. The players were chosen by former captain of England, Mike

Brearley and some were even brought from as far away as Australia. There was television coverage and a good crowd to witness this most unusual 'match'. Graham Gooch had not read the rules and tried to leave the pitch too soon, whereupon Christopher had to stop him or he would have been disqualified. The television homed in on this incident and Gooch eventually returned to complete his innings. Clive Lloyd, that outstanding West Indian, won the competition off Michael Holding's bowling. It was more than a memorable occasion for Christopher as he had been partly responsible for its creation.

Christopher has two books to his credit, both about cricket. *Think Cricket*, published in 2001, which is an indispensable aid to coaches, and *Plan Cricket*, which no self-respecting cricket club should be without, in 2003. As if this was not enough, he is a tireless fundraiser – on one occasion he raised £5,000 in a single game. Has he any plans to retire and put his feet up? Not at the moment. Gette simply wants more of the same. More writing (he now writes for *Cricket World*) and more cricket for as long as possible. His life suits him just the way it is.

Christopher David Evelyn Bazalgette
b. 24th November 1938, Edgbaston, England
Left hand bat
Slow medium away swing, flight and guile

J. D. Hull's Drillers XI v The Bat and Ball Cricket Club, Broadhalfpenny Down, near Hambledon
from an oil painting by Jocelyn Galsworthy